'It's a handbook that provides intelligent, highly effective, practical approaches to understanding young people who set fires. Foster writes with warmth and passion giving insightful, sensitive advice grounded in a caring, child-centred philosophy that will be beneficial to anyone who works with vulnerable young people. A must read for educators everywhere. This book has the power to save lives.'

– *Tamsin Winter, author of* Being Miss Nobody *and* Jemima Small Versus the Universe

* * * * *

'Joanna Foster has done a wonderful job of producing a highly accessible text that introduces the reader to best practice in fire safety work with children and young people. This book is highly engaging and should be essential reading for those tasked with the difficult job of addressing firesetting in children and young people.'

– *Professor Theresa A. Gannon, Director of Centre of Research and Education in Forensic Psychology, University of Kent*

* * * * *

'What a wonderful read. The author's warmth, care, love and commitment to this important area of work is evident in every word on the page. The book is informative and provides a great deal of insight into the area of firesetting. This book generously provides practitioners with practical tools, confidence and inspiration to undertake work in this area. The exercises are brilliant in their simplicity and are transferable to a variety of other disciplines. A superb book.'

– *Roz Morrison, former assistant chief probation officer and currently senior lecturer at De Montfort University*

CHILDREN AND TEENAGERS
WHO SET FIRES

Children and Teenagers Who Set Fires

Why They Do It and How to Help

Joanna E. Foster
Foreword by Professor David Kolko

Jessica Kingsley *Publishers*
London and Philadelphia

Every effort has been made to trace copyright holders and to obtain their permission for the use of copyright material where necessary. The author and the publisher apologise for any omissions and would be grateful if notified of any acknowledgements that should be incorporated in future reprints or editions of this book.

First published in 2020
by Jessica Kingsley Publishers
73 Collier Street
London N1 9BE, UK
and
400 Market Street, Suite 400
Philadelphia, PA 19106, USA

www.jkp.com

Library of Congress Cataloging in Publication Data
A CIP catalog record for this book is available from the Library of Congress

British Library Cataloguing in Publication Data
A CIP catalogue record for this book is available from the British Library

ISBN 978 1 78592 533 7
eISBN 978 1 78450 929 3

Printed and bound in Great Britain

This book is dedicated to Jenny-Lee, whose only voice was fire.
She is forever an inspiration on the possibility of change.

Contents

Foreword

As a practitioner and researcher who has worked with children and adolescents involved in the misuse of fire for more than 40 years, it is a privilege to write this foreword for *Children and Teenagers Who Set Fires: Why They Do It and How to Help*, written by my friend and colleague, Joanna Foster. Children and young people are often naturally curious about fire and experience it in a positive way from an early age, such as a campfire or home barbecue. For most children and adolescents, this exposure begins a long history of responsible contact with fire that is generally safe and beneficial. However, for others, the use of fire may result in more adverse and dangerous consequences due to their limited understanding as to how to control it, or their explicit desire to use it for more destructive purposes.

There are various books, technical reports, scientific articles, and program resources or materials to address the issue of youth firesetting behaviour. In part, this is due to the fact that the unsanctioned use of fire by children and adolescents is a significant public health problem in many countries, especially in North America and Europe. In the USA alone, this problem is associated with thousands of fires each year, causing significant loss of life and injuries, millions of dollars in property damage, and many other consequences, including family despair, disruption of daily routines and loss of insurance. The lack of equivalent data for the UK is highlighted in this book, raising the bold question of how seriously youth firesetting is taken by policy makers and budget holders.

This new book is the only resource devoted entirely to the topic of child and adolescent firesetting from the perspective of a professional working in the UK. In fact, there are very few professional resources written on this topic from any perspective. The book includes nine chapters that cover a range of topics focusing on the prevalence and significance of juvenile firesetting, the various motives for – and contributors to – the desire to set a fire across age ranges, and some of the broader reasons for, or causes of, a firesetting incident. This information provides a normative and societal context for understanding the nature of the problem, and some of the ways in which help for this problem is desperately needed. The book also covers an overview of interventions that have been found to be effective in addressing this problem, since there are reports of the use of methods that are less than beneficial or ethical that circulate in the field, such as the use of shock tactics and punitive approaches.

Three chapters focus on methods for use with very young children, school-aged children, and then adolescents. Each one highlights some of the more well-documented intervention approaches that have been evaluated, including fire safety education and cognitive behavioural therapy. Of course, as noted in the book, not all children receive psychosocial approaches and this response in the UK is taken far less routinely. Each chapter also introduces and applies some key components or strategies to enhance learning fire safety concepts or encourage adoption of a new behavioural response or skill. An additional chapter focuses on how to adapt these approaches and strategies to the needs of youth with intellectual or developmental challenges who require more creative solutions. This is illustrated in several case examples that highlight some of the diverse child, parental, family, and neighbourhood characteristics that may be found among these cases which require nimble case conceptualisations and integrative case planning and intervention delivery.

Finally, a signature chapter outlines the creative and extensive intervention that was used with 13-year-old Jenny-Lee, who received support after setting fires in a flat within a high-rise building. The case highlights numerous features common in the backgrounds and histories of children who set fires, and the intervention that took place highlights a number of novel but fascinating details and issues. Several appendices also provide additional materials relevant to serving this population in a planned and accountable manner.

This book should be of great interest to both professionals and parents, who will find its insights and suggestions to have practical value. It also incorporates the front-line and managerial experiences of a talented practitioner with a keen sense for delivering tailored recommendations and services. Thus, it uniquely integrates both art and science in an effort to support a compassionate perspective for working with this challenging but needy child and adolescent population.

Professor David Kolko
University of Pittsburgh School of Medicine

Acknowledgements

My early flourishing in this field of work would not have been possible without three very wise men whose professionalism, knowledge and integrity have made me a better practitioner: Professor David Kolko of the University of Pittsburgh, Director Robin Morris-Jones of the Cognitive Centre and Group Manager Stuart McMillan of the London Fire Brigade (now retired). Between them they ensured my sanity and wellbeing as they strived to protect the protector.

Above these towering strengths are my parents, who give me wings to fly, a safety net for the times I fall, and unending, unconditional, boundless love that makes everything I've achieved possible.

Alongside an army of close friends too gifted and brilliant and numerous to mention, I also give my humblest of thanks to the hundreds of children and families that have allowed me to enter into their lives at often the worst of times. It has always been a privilege to walk alongside you.

As for the team at Jessica Kingsley Publishers, I continue to pinch myself daily at having been approached by them to write this work. Everyone does indeed have a book inside them.

And last, but never least, my love and thanks to my husband Imanol. He knows what for.

Preface

A Note of Encouragement from the Author

It would be untrue to say I always dreamed of working with children and teenagers who set fires. It was never amongst the list of job options offered by the Careers Officer at Aberdare Girls' Comprehensive School, and it certainly wasn't an obvious choice for a history graduate of Magdalen College, Oxford.

Yet just as the study of history seeks to best understand how we have reached a certain point in time, so the same sense of curiosity must be shown towards the child or teenager who is setting fires. Be it the toddler playing persistently with a lighter or the teenager seemingly intent upon causing destruction through fire, in order to find out their story we, as professionals, parents and members of a shared society, must ask ourselves: 'How did we let our children get to this point?' For firesetting behaviour by children and young people can be devastating and its potential for harm should not be underestimated. Those faced with dealing with the problem can feel overwhelmed, despairing and ill-equipped. Are parents' worst fears of having raised a 'monster' realised when a child sets fire? Are professionals faced with few options but to mark these children as dangerous, both to themselves and others?

Over the course of this book I aim to help you unpick what is meant by 'juvenile firesetting behaviour', understand why a child or teenager might set fires, and introduce you to the strategies I have used in my practice for nearly two decades. These hands-on activities have allowed me to give my clients the focused attention all our children and young people deserve. This has in turn helped enable them to find a voice other than fire. I am confident that with practice and patience, these often easy-to-replicate techniques can do the same for you and the child you are supporting. There isn't a strategy in these pages that I am not confident about, because I am not here to make you fail or make myself seem cleverer. I want to inspire you with the same passion I have for this work and allow you to realise the best you can be when supporting a child who is setting fires.

The case studies featured throughout this book are used to illustrate the different ways strategies can be used and to remind us that behind every child-set fire is a personal, human story deserving of being heard. My anonymised practice examples have at times been blended and certain identifying details changed to respect the privacy of all the families I work with. What hasn't been changed is the bravery of every child and family that accepts help, especially when trusting professionals is often so very difficult because of previous experiences of not being seen, heard or understood. I hope that by hearing these voices you will be inspired about the potential and change that is possible. It is up to you to decide which specific activities to use with a child or teenager and when. Where suggestions are provided on the questions to ask, you will find your own words to convey and teach the skills and ideas being explored. If you are a practitioner, I hope this book will enable you to see the hope and privilege that lie at the heart of our work. If you are a parent, be kind to yourself for you are doing the hardest job. Chances are as a parent or practitioner you're having a pretty tough time right now, but I hope this book will allow you to see the greatness that exists in every child; it's there, waiting for you to unleash it.

Resources in the appendices and any pages marked with a * can be downloaded from www.jkp.com/catalogue/book/9781785925337 for your own personal use.

CHAPTER 1

What Exactly Is Juvenile Firesetting Behaviour?

That is the question.

When talking about children and teenagers who set fires, you will hear terms like 'juvenile firesetting', 'deliberate firesetting', 'arsonist' and even 'pyromaniac'. These sometimes vague and often incorrectly used terms can make it a minefield for a parent or practitioner to understand exactly what a child is doing and why they are doing it.

To help, we'll assign to the dustbin immediately the less useful descriptions you'll hear about children and teenagers who set fires, be it in newspapers and on television, on social media or from the mouths of colleagues and family members; descriptions such as:

FIREBUG WHO TORCHED A CHURCH

YOBS SET FIRE TO ORCHARD PARK BEAUTY SPOT

THE MAKING OF A FIRE-STARTER

These headline quotes, taken directly from various UK media sources, have all been used to describe children and teenagers who set fires (Crow 2019; BBC news online 2011; Hanlon 2009, respectively). The dramatic headlines seek to deliberately ignite our interest and enflame our emotions (all puns intended), and in doing so successfully draw attention away from the reality that these firebugs, (twisted) fire-starters and yobs are *children* and *teenagers*, who – like the rest of us – are all more deserving, complicated and layered than a single derisory label.

With lazy, ill-informed stereotypes thus binned there are other words that we will remove from the vocabulary of this book. I will also avoid the terms 'arson' and 'arsonist'. This is not to say that young people do not commit arson, and it is more than possible that as a practitioner you may be working with a young person who has been charged with arson. However, I want to leave aside this terminology for two reasons. First, our work is enhanced when we see a young person as an individual, rather than in blanket terms such as 'arsonist'; and second, as the act of arson has to fit a specific legal definition, I do not want to exclude from our attention those children and teenagers who are setting fires but have not come into contact with the youth justice system. The action of setting fires by children and young people should not be treated any less seriously simply because they have not been charged with arson, because the more we can do early on to stop this behaviour and prevent it escalating to the point where it requires statutory intervention, the better. I have sat in on too many child protection and youth offending team meetings where concerns for this behaviour could have been prevented by the simplest of remedial actions: namely, adults removing the potential risk and harm of fire by making matches and lighters inaccessible to children, which we will explore further in Chapter 2.

Alongside 'arsonist', any reference to the disorder pyromania (as defined in the *Diagnostic Statistical Manual version 5 (DSM-5)*, American Psychiatric Association 2013) will also not be used. Despite very many people proclaiming, upon hearing what I do, 'Oh, you work with little pyromaniacs!' (cue eyeroll from me), pyromania is rarely diagnosed and is under-researched in both adults and children (Ó Ciardha, Tyler and Gannon 2017). In 16 years of practice I have never worked with a child who has been diagnosed with the disorder. Given the number of exclusion criteria within *DSM-5* preventing the diagnosis of pyromania – including a diagnosis of conduct disorder, ideological convictions (such as terrorist or political beliefs), anger or revenge, a desire to cover up another crime, impaired judgement as a result of substance misuse or a learning disability – it is difficult to imagine a scenario where a child or teenager could be classified as a pyromaniac. Therefore, it is not simply sensitivity to labels but also a desire to be accurate and evidence based that explains why the term pyromaniac will not be used in this book.

Thus, we are left considering the definition of the term most frequently used in academic literature, clinical research and by practitioners (myself included): that of 'juvenile firesetting'. Despite this largely accepted term, caution is again needed in its application and meaning for there is no single, universally agreed definition of its meaning. Ethically, branding a child or teenager as a 'firesetter' can be as limiting and damaging as 'arsonist' or 'pyromaniac', because there is a genuine concern about whether the criteria for firesetting in one study are comparable to those in other studies (Mehregany 1993). Therefore, are we even talking about the same thing when we casually use the word 'firesetter'? If we start to consider the definitions for the 'type' of firesetter a child or teenager might be, the world of words becomes even murkier.

Research studies tell us about the 'delinquent' or 'severely disturbed' juvenile firesetter (Wooden and Berkey 1984) alongside the 'pathological', 'non-pathological' and 'cognitively impaired' firesetter (Slavkin and Fineman 2000). Whilst these terms can be useful to help us make sense of theory, without due care or context these classifications applied to the children and teenagers we work with could cause confusion at best and harm at worst. I cannot begin to imagine how it would feel to be the child or parent that lives with the description 'severely disturbed firesetter', or how you define your sense of self if as an adult you attend treatment entitled 'Firesetting Intervention Programme for Mentally Disordered Offenders' (FIPMO; see Gannon and Lockerbie 2014).

My extreme caution in the use of our words is neither to undermine nor disagree with the importance and validity of research and treatment programmes in this field. Classifications of firesetting behaviour are attempting to establish the motives for the setting of fires and are therefore useful in thinking about how we best respond; a young child setting fires out of curiosity about what might happen next is likely to require a different response to the older teenager who wants to cause harm through fire – it's the whole premise for this book. My caution is simply a nod to the power of words and the fact that language matters, especially when used by people in power. Considering that adults are usually the ones holding the power in relationships with children, every word we use matters. At its simplest, put aside any diagnosis or psychological term when describing a child or teenager; using a child's name when having to talk about them and what they're doing is not only politer but is often far more accurate than describing a person by a definition or disorder.

Definition of juvenile firesetting

For the purposes of this book and to ensure we have a shared understanding of what we're talking about as we explore together ways of working with this behaviour, I'll define juvenile firesetting as follows:

The unsanctioned use of fire by a child or teenager.

To be even more blunt about it, we're talking about *fires that children and teenagers should not be having*, because of the potential danger posed to them and others.

I've placed emphasis on the 'unsanctioned use' of fire because

I am not concerned about those children who are taught safe, age-appropriate use of fire by a responsible adult. If we want to nurture the growth of confident young adults who can fend for themselves and are not living a 'battery-hen life' (Children's Commissioner Anne Longfield in *The Observer*, 2018), then the need for outdoor adventures and the teaching of cooking skills for children of all genders is to be encouraged. Instead, this book is about supporting those children who are playing with fire, or setting fires, without the permission or supervision of a responsible adult, regardless of any intention to cause harm or damage.

CHAPTER 2

Whose Problem and Who's Listening?

Now that we've established the behaviour that we're talking about, I'd like to provide a note of reassurance to parents and practitioners alike about the children and teenagers who set fires. In my years of direct work with this group of people, I wouldn't consider any of them as 'mad', 'bad' or beyond hope. Yes, they are often feeling sad, hurt and fearful: emotions that are expressed in seemingly 'crazy', 'wrong' and sometimes even frightening actions that are destructive and violent (as much to themselves as to others). Yet understanding this problematic behaviour is much more about recognising what's happening *to* a child, as opposed to what's wrong with them.

Firesetting as a form of communication

In his 2013 autobiography entitled *Mini and Me*, Michael 'Mini' Cooper – who from the age of 10 was deemed too dangerous to live in the community because of fires he had set at home and in a local church, and was kept incarcerated in secure accommodation until a young adult – explains that he set fires because it was his only voice. Mini says, 'I was so very young, yet wanted to scream like an adult, wanted that power and strength but I couldn't articulate any of this without the matches' (p.20). In reading Mini's autobiography, you learn he inhabited a terrifying world of domestic abuse at home and harsh physical violence in his religious school. The clues were there in what Mini was setting fire to.

'Listening' to firesetting behaviour – Lisa's story

Fourteen-year-old Lisa lived at home with her mother and younger brother. An intelligent and high-performing student, she had begun to self-harm, set fires and perform less well at school. When working with Lisa, she justified her firesetting by explaining that whilst some teenagers drink and take drugs, her 'thing' was fire. Despite the physical freedoms associated with being a teenager, Lisa's firesetting never took place outside but was always carried out at home. Two particular incidents of firesetting at home stood out for me because of the destruction and response they caused; the first involved Lisa spraying her bedroom door with an aerosol and setting it alight (causing damage to the door) and the second was when Lisa lit a sparkler, resulting in a visible burn mark to the light-coloured living room carpet. The damage to Lisa's home, which was otherwise *immaculately* kept, caused a great deal of upset to her mother.

Knowing this had been Mum's reaction, in one of my fire safety sessions with Lisa I pre-prepared a series of sticky notes listing words and phrases that could be considered possible reasons for a young person to set fires. These included:

CURIOUS   BORED   FASCINATED   EXCITED

I LIKE THE FLAMES   IT GETS MUM'S ATTENTION   FOR FUN

EVERYONE DOES IT   WHERE'S THE HARM?   LONELY

Spreading all the sticky notes out on the table, I asked Lisa to point to any words that reflected her reasons for setting fires. Lisa pointed to the note that read 'It gets Mum's attention'.

This allowed me to explore with Lisa in what ways she felt she didn't get her mother's attention, and ideas on how her mum could give her this. Lisa asked for time alone with Mum away from her younger brother (who because of his age demanded more of Mum's attention). It was as simple as that. With Lisa's permission I discussed our conversation with her mum, who was devastated to learn that her daughter needed to set fires in order to get her attention.

Mum felt she had failed in her role as a mother to keep her daughter safe, yet the reality was that she was a single mother of two children who was running a busy home and was also a carer for her own mother. Alongside her demanding and stressful life as a carer across generations, as a second-generation immigrant to the UK, Mum was also juggling the often conflicting cultural attitudes between her own mother and daughter on what were considered acceptable behaviours for teenage girls. All this had led Mum to feel torn between pleasing her mother and making her daughter happy, and amongst it all she had forgotten that her clever, competent and capable teenage daughter still needed quality time alone with her in order to feel accepted and loved. For as well as emotional attention, physical closeness between mother and daughter had also become increasingly absent.

Due to the anger felt by Mum about the firesetting, it had been some time since she had hugged Lisa. This universal declaration of reassurance and acceptance had fallen out of Mum's repertoire through sheer exasperation at her daughter's behaviour. In my conversations with Mum I negotiated mother and daughter time for her and Lisa, and suggested reintroducing hugs, encouraging Mum to keep giving them even if Lisa shrugged them off initially. Steadily, time getting their nails done together began to happen, hugs were gradually and consistently re-introduced, and Lisa was given safe responsibility around fire in the form of helping Mum prepare and cook hot meals for the family some evenings. This freed up some of Mum's time as a carer, sent a message to Lisa that she was trusted, and allowed Mum to recognise the increasingly independent, responsible and sensible teenager she had raised. Alongside the fire safety education I delivered in our sessions together, through counselling arranged via the family GP Lisa was able to explore the reasons for her self-harm. Gradually, Lisa began to identify other ways of coping with, and communicating, her emotions.

Fast forward nine years and Lisa is a law graduate, master's student, proud feminist and mental health blogger who enjoys a strong, close and loving relationship with both her mother and grandmother. As for her mother, she's deservedly proud of both the grown-up children she raised and nurtured single-handedly.

Mini and Lisa's need to be heard teaches us just how crucial it is to recognise the setting of fires as a form of communication. As adults it is our job to work out what it is that children and teenagers are telling us through their actions. What is it that we 'grown-ups' just aren't hearing or seeing that it takes the setting of fires (or any other kind of destructive behaviour) to make us sit up and take notice of a child and their world? When children's and teenagers' behaviour becomes dangerous and damaging, are we guilty of listening less when we should be listening all the more?

The adult's role

As we start to consider what might be going on for our children and teenagers that helps explain their firesetting, now is a good time to introduce the work of Professor David J. Kolko. Remember that name, not simply because he will appear more than once in this book but because if you're a practitioner wanting to read more about clinical and treatment interventions for adolescent firesetters in particular, his are the books and papers to be aware of. Professor of Psychiatry, Psychology and Paediatrics at the University of Pittsburgh School of Medicine and Director of the Special Services Unit at the Western Psychiatric Unit and Clinic, Professor Kolko has dedicated over 40 years of practice to the research and treatment of children who set fires. His writings inform (and inspire) much of my everyday work. Of everything that I have learned from Professor Kolko and will share with you in these pages, it is a statement he made at a UK conference in 2015 that I want us to always hold on to as we attempt to understand juvenile firesetting. Addressing a national firesetting conference, Professor Kolko encouraged a packed room of professionals from across the fields of fire safety, psychology and social care to always be mindful that just as child abuse is a problem with adult behaviour, *firesetting by children is a problem resulting from adult behaviour.*

Let's think about this a little more. If you're a teenager setting fires, what about the responsibility sitting with the adult that sold you your ignition materials? With no minimum age requirement in the UK for the purchase of lighters and matches, what are we expecting teenagers to do with any lighters they have, especially as it is illegal to buy cigarettes below the age of 18? In recognition that some teenagers may indeed be buying lighters and matches for the purpose of setting fires, South Yorkshire Fire and Rescue service ran a campaign entitled 'Strike it Out' in 2011 (BBC news online 2011), urging local retailers to voluntarily sign up to banning the sale of lighters and matches to anyone under the age of 18 over the Hallowe'en and Bonfire Night periods. Recognising that a teenager with a lighter raises questions about the responsibility of adults and their actions, at the younger end of the childhood spectrum we must similarly consider the role of the carer that didn't stop the toddler from turning on the cooker or playing with a lighter.

If you're reading this as a parent, this isn't to say the firesetting is your fault. You can't know 24-7 what your children are doing, even when they're under the same roof as you. I stress our role as the responsible adults because too often what we see as 'naughty behaviour' is nothing more than a child being curious and needing our attention. The infant playing with fire will stop as soon as we take away the lighters and matches they're using (I haven't had a referral yet for a child setting fires by rubbing two sticks together). No clinical assessment or cognitive therapy is needed for a toddler setting fires, just remove the opportunity. It's as simple as that. And when parenting is the hardest job, let's bring on all the quick fixes we can get.

Curious Kharis

When little ones go suspiciously quiet for too long this is often a good sign that they've discovered something they shouldn't be doing, succeeding in their role of curious beings seeking out new and interesting things regardless of how dangerous those new and interesting things may be. Five-year-old Shireen and 3-year-old Kharis had been noisily playing together when their mum became suspicious at how quiet both children had become. On entering their bedroom, Mum found the curtains alight and both children hiding under the bed. Mum grabbed the children, left the house and called 999. Kharis later admitted that she had been playing with the lighter that was usually left on the cooker in the kitchen.

With the role of adults thus established as being instrumental in causing – and solving – the problem of child-set fires, so we need to think about the family environment as a further backstory to the fires being set.

CHAPTER 3

Why Does It Happen?

Firesetting behaviour by children does not happen in a vacuum and the research of Professor Kolko highlights that it is crucial to 'think family' when considering the context of juvenile firesetting behaviour. The parents of children and teenagers who set fires report higher levels of personal or relationship problems (such as conflict between partners) and greater difficulties with parenting practices – including supervising and setting boundaries for their children – than parents whose children do not set fires (Kazdin and Kolko 1986; Kolko and Kazdin 1990; Kolko and Kazdin 1992). Looking beyond the issues of supervision and boundaries, at a wider family level children and teenagers setting fires have been found to 'experience more stressful life events' than those who do not set fires (Kolko 2002, p.42).

A response to stressful life events

It would be difficult to imagine a 21st-century family that does not experience stress at some point: that feeling of being under too much emotional and mental pressure. Whilst people have different ways of reacting to stress – whereby a situation that feels stressful to one person may indeed prove motivating to another – there are certain incidents we experience that can safely be considered as stressful life events for most of us and definitely for our children. These are the death of a loved one, separation and divorce, and moving to a new home. In these circumstances, the firesetting can reflect the need for adult attention and help in dealing with a recent crisis (Wooden and Berkey 1984), as was the case for Liam, Craig and Megan.

Loss of a loved one

Ten-year-old Liam's father had died when he was 9 and his sister was 12. Since the death of their father, Liam's behaviour had become disruptive in class and his older sister was refusing to go outside. Liam had also started to set fires at home and in the garden.

Mum joined me in all my sessions with Liam, which were held at school to allow for some consistency in his usual routine. This predictability was vital when so many other parts of life had changed beyond all recognition and imagination for Liam. Most of our sessions involved reading children's fire safety books together and playing board games. As Liam learned through play the important difference between good and bad fires, equally crucial in our work was his time spent playing with Mum. Just playing together. Whilst our sessions could never erase the grief and loss the family was experiencing, it provided time and a space where having fun and laughing was allowed and encouraged, something that had been largely missing at home for over a year.

Separation

Eleven-year-old Craig's parents had recently separated. His mother had moved out of the family home and whilst Craig was meant to stay with Mum every weekend, this was often disrupted due to Dad's refusal to let him and his two siblings

---

see their mother on the grounds of her physical ill-health. Craig set a fire in the living room, which Dad extinguished and mentioned to Craig's social worker as evidence of how 'bad' Craig was. Craig was being supported by a social worker and a play therapist due to neglect suffered at home.

During one session together in the spring, Craig asked me who he would be spending Christmas with – Mum or Dad. Despite Christmas being nine months away, the reality of the family's first Christmas spent apart was on his mind. I explained and apologised to Craig that I didn't know the answer to this question and we spent some time drawing out on paper ideas about who can help us with questions, especially difficult ones that worry us. After completing this exercise, I used his question to consider how we could help make his Christmas feel fire-safe whichever home he would be in. A discussion ensued about never playing with fire, testing smoke alarms and not burning food, which his grandmother often did when he lived with her. Talking about time spent with his grandmother was a happy memory for Craig.

Moving home

I was asked to offer advice on the case of 15-year-old Megan who had begun to set fires, behaviour considered completely out of character for her. Megan was described to me as having Asperger Syndrome, a form of autism, and had lived at home with her adoptive parents since the age of 3. After just a few questions about Megan's adoptive family, including who else lived at home, I established that Megan's older sister (her birth sister who had been adopted together with Megan) had been offered a job working away, meaning that she would be leaving the family home for the first time.

Amidst the family's celebrations of her success, including by Megan, no one had considered the negative impact the move might signify for her. It is reasonable to imagine she would struggle with this change because of her Asperger Syndrome (routine is crucial for all children to help them feel safe and comfortable but especially for children with Asperger Syndrome, who can find change distressing), her previous experience of loss when separated from her birth parents, and as a sibling coming to terms with missing an older sister whom she loved. I suggested asking Megan what she thought about her sister moving away. (Notice the slightly different emphasis here; it can sometimes be more difficult for people with autism to express and understand emotions and so asking what they are thinking, rather than feeling, can offer an easier way to articulate what's going on in a way that is more accessible than the trickiness of emotions.)

It became apparent that Megan was anxious about her sister's move, and had troubling questions about where she would be living, who she would be living with and what she would be doing every day. Megan's sister was happy with my suggestion to spend time with her looking at photographs of her new city, her new flat and the office she would be working in. She also agreed to draw up a timetable for Megan so that she knew what her week would entail and what day she would call her. This preparation and planning allowed Megan to feel less anxious about the major change ahead and enabled her to feel a part of it, agreeing to help with the packing and the move on the big day.

Liam, Craig and Megan's firesetting was their way of communicating that life events were becoming too difficult to deal with. Finding out as much as possible about each of them allowed me to realise that their firesetting was a symptom of something else happening in their lives, which was too big, difficult and painful to communicate through words. Be it consciously or unconsciously, by setting fires each of them was able to command the attention of different adults around them because *it's really difficult to ignore fires and those who start them*. What some may describe as attention-seeking behaviour by Craig, Liam and Megan (and Mini and Lisa in Chapter 2), I prefer to think of it as *attachment-seeking* behaviour. These children and teenagers were reaching out to adults to help them navigate through life's painful and difficult journey. Therefore, I always consider the following hypothesis (proposed explanation) whenever I am first told about any child setting fires – this child is setting fires to say *something*.

Firesetting out of curiosity or boredom

For very young children, it's a reasonable hypothesis that what is being said when they set fires is 'I'm curious!' One of the most common reasons mentioned by children for setting fires is curiosity, especially amongst children aged 2 to 7 (Kolko and Vernberg 2017). This is of little surprise, given that children are naturally curious creatures, wondering, exploring and questioning *everything*. It is this curiosity that drives their development and I often think that fire must seem especially magical to very young children as flames change shape and colour with a sound, smell, taste and warmth that stimulate all of their five senses. When children are curious about something they want to explore it, often again and again, which means that a very young child playing with fire even more than once is rarely looking to cause harm but is simply discovering what it's all about in the easiest way they know how – by touching and playing. The same can even be said of teenagers whose curiosity, piqued by what they've seen in science class or on social media, leads them to experiment with fire in their bedrooms or back gardens without thinking through all the potential risks and dangers of what they are doing.

Therefore, whilst it is important to hypothesise over what a child's firesetting is saying, we must ensure that we follow the evidence we get in response to our questions about a child and their family, and ensure we do not invent problems that don't exist. Sometimes the firesetting really is about nothing more than being curious, bored and having fun, the three most frequent reasons given for firesetting as reported in a large school survey of Canadian pupils in grades 1 (age 6–7) to 12 (age 17–18). This same study also established that less than 10 per cent of the children setting fires gave reasons of anger or the desire to hurt someone (Cotterall, McPhee and Plecas 1999) so it is vital that we do not 'pathologise' or 'medicalise' the problem of juvenile firesetting. That is, we must not regard or treat firesetting as psychologically abnormal when it is simply a child's way of responding to their environment or something that is happening to them.

Other reasons for firesetting

When a child or teenager's firesetting is motivated by factors other than boredom, play or curiosity, the reasons can be many and varied. These can include, but are not limited to, copycat behaviour (Lambie, Randell and McDowell 2013), a reflection of more generalised involvement in antisocial behaviour (Wooden and Berkey 1984), anger, retaliation, pressure from peers and friends, and reacting to something bad that has happened (Kolko and Vernberg 2017). Again, none of these suggest that there is a problem with the child but are potential indicators that all is not well within the environment they find themselves in. It is also important to remember that a child's reason for setting one fire could be very different to their motivation for the next fire they set, and there is room for overlap; it doesn't take a huge stretch of the imagination to realise it's very possible for a child to be bored, unsupervised *and* then curious about the lighter they've seen used so many times. Thus, like children and teenagers, we must be curious about the child or teenager setting fires and explore all possible reasons for their motives, never discounting any potential reasons from our hypotheses until the evidence suggests otherwise. Remaining open to all the possibilities, we especially never dismiss or explain away juvenile firesetting behaviour because of a child's gender or where they are from.

Boys will be boys?

Despite it being an uncommon occurrence, I am still shocked when a practitioner – often working for a fire service – attributes a child's firesetting to the fact that they are a boy or because of where they live. Unless a whole body of research and evidence has passed me by, I'm really not aware that a child is destined to set fires either because they're male or happen to live in a certain area, usually a deprived one. There is nothing pre-determined about firesetting behaviour, and seeing it as 'normal' because a child is male or from a less affluent area says far more about us and our ill-conceived misconceptions about gender and potential than it does about any child and where they live. Do we really not expect better of boys and children living in poverty?

An example of this kind of prejudice was the case of a young boy who had set a fire at home but had not been referred for fire safety education by the fire crew that attended the property to put out the fire. When I asked the Officer in Charge at the fire why the information hadn't been shared, I was greeted with the explanation, 'Well, if we refer him, we'll be referring every kid on that street.' Needless to say, the officer spent the remainder of his afternoon completing referral forms for this boy and every other home he had ever attended for a child-set fire on 'that' street.

This isn't to deny that juvenile firesetting is carried out by more boys than girls. As with other externalising antisocial behaviours, boys are consistently shown to be more likely to exhibit firesetting behaviour, with a prevalence of around two to three times that of girls across a range of samples of children in the community (Chen, Arria and Anthony 2003; Dadds and Fraser 2006; Del Bove *et al.* 2008; Martin *et al.* 2004). Yet to either accept or excuse a child's firesetting on the grounds of their gender risks both ignoring the problem and what might be being 'said' by the behaviour.

It is similarly realistic to acknowledge that there are within our towns and cities crime 'hotspots', with an emerging body of research interested in developing a more integrated understanding of what is termed 'geographical criminology' (Bottoms 2012; Weisburd, Groff and Yang 2012; Wikström *et al.* 2012). Therefore, there will absolutely be areas where levels of deliberately set fires are higher than found elsewhere, including those set by children and young people. Yet setting and space alone cannot explain – nor make acceptable – a child's firesetting. If we start to expect little better of our children and teenagers from 'that street', 'that estate' and 'that family', we can easily begin to think that there is little hope for change or better outcomes for our families. We could start to believe that nothing works.

CHAPTER 4

What Works?

The 'What works?' question plagues most frontline practitioners and particularly so since the 1970s, when rehabilitation and behaviour change work lost much of its legitimacy. This was largely due to a now infamous article by US sociologist Robert Martinson, which posed the question 'What works?' regarding prison reform (Martinson 1974). Despite evidencing some successes, Martinson's became the defining voice for a generation that concluded *nothing works* and ushered in a loss of faith in rehabilitation 'akin to a stock market crash' (Garland 2001, p.69). Attempting to reverse the damage done to rehabilitative services, the intervening decades have seen concerted efforts across various disciplines to evidence that accepted interventions and strategies in mental health and behaviour change are indeed effective and can 'work'. Governments around the world, healthcare systems and policymakers have decided that quality of care should improve, it should be evidence based, and that it is in the public's interest to ensure this happens (Barlow 2004; Weisz and Kazdin 2017).

However, despite this emphasis on research-led practice, large gaps remain in evidencing what works in addressing juvenile firesetting behaviour. Frustratingly, the volume of work by practitioners and the rich experience base that has developed 'far exceeds the availability of new scientific studies and clinical reports in this area' (Kolko and Foster 2017, p.98), particularly within the UK. Yet perhaps it is little wonder that an evidence-based theoretical model for this work does not exist in the UK, because we have no idea of the scale of the problem we are facing. *No national data exists on the number of fires set by children and teenagers each year.* Nothing. Absolutely nothing. In the USA it is reported that between the years 2007 and 2011 children set an average of 49,300 fires, causing 80 deaths, 860 injuries and property damage estimated at $235 million per annum (Campbell 2014) yet no equivalent figures are available for the UK in any given period. Whether we look at the annual fire statistics for each of the four nations of the UK individually or collectively, no records are available to provide illumination on the magnitude of the problem of juvenile firesetting.

In the Welsh language the word 'dim' means nothing or no. In the English language, it means to not see brightly or clearly. Therefore, I can think of no better phrase to use than 'dim data' when it comes to describing the evidence available for juvenile firesetting in the UK. In the face of 'dim data' how do we even begin to adequately support families and communities, resource staff appropriately, respond meaningfully and evaluate effectively? As practitioners, how can we possibly hope for 'evidence of any systematic approach' (Palmer, Caulfield and Hollin 2005, p.40) or clarity on what works when nobody really knows the scale of what we are tackling?

The evidence base for what works

The current UK landscape mirrors the scene Professor Kolko faced nearly 40 years ago in the USA when he accepted his first referral for a young child that had set a fire at home. Virtually no empirical literature on juvenile firesetting was available and there were no evidence-supported guidelines for addressing the behaviour. Recognising the absences that needed to be addressed, Kolko began to secure grants and collaborate with other agencies in order to conduct and publish scientific studies on the description, assessment, follow-up and treatment of these children and teenagers. Thus, a knowledge base in this field began to grow and with it the materials and methods 'found to work' (Kolko and Vernberg 2017, p.xiii). Given that the ongoing gaps in UK evidence are similar to those that Kolko identified almost four decades ago in the USA, I look to his, and others', findings over the intervening years to ground my practice as best as possible in an evidence base of what works with children and teenagers who set fires.

First, the *Handbook on Firesetting in Children and Youth*, edited by Kolko and published in 2002, is my 'bible' for this work (it always makes me smile that an atheist – that's me – is describing a book edited by a Jew – that's Kolko – as a bible; I think that's what they call 'life's rich tapestry'). With chapters that cover areas including historical perspectives, developmental dimensions, screening and triage tools, and clinical assessments, Chapter 10 focuses on fire safety education. Written by Irene Pinsonneault of the Massachusetts Statewide Coalition for Juvenile Firesetter Intervention Programs, the chapter describes fire safety education as the 'primary intervention process for all types of firesetting behaviour' (p.223) and goes on to list four studies that provide evidence of fire safety education as effective in reducing firesetting by children and teenagers (DeSalvatore and Hornstein 1991; Kolko 1996; Lasden 1987; Webb, Sakheim and Towns-Miranda 1990).

Pinsonneault is not alone in her emphasis on the potency of fire safety education. The need for such an approach as a 'first step in the treatment of firesetting behaviour' (Lambie, Ioane and Randell 2016, p.34) echoes across research carried out outside of the UK. No matter the severity of the firesetting behaviour, education-based interventions are highly recommended as a mandatory component of treatment for all children and teenagers who set fires (Lambie and Randell 2011; Stadolnik 2000). Fire safety education approaches aim to increase fire knowledge, encourage fire-safe behaviours and teach children, teenagers and their families the strategies needed for staying safe from fire, which have been evidenced to reduce repeat firesetting and fire-related behaviour (Franklin *et al.* 2002; Kolko 2001; Kolko, Watson and Faust 1991).

In his 2001 study cited above, Kolko compared the three most common interventions for juvenile firesetting behaviour – community-based fire safety education (FSE) programmes, cognitive behavioural therapy (CBT) delivered by mental health practitioners, and a single home visit from a firefighter (HVF). Although all three approaches showed improvements in measures of fire involvement, fire interest and fire risk, longer-term FSE and CBT interventions were more effective than a one-off HVF in reducing the frequency of firesetting, the number of children who later played with matches, a child's involvement in fire-related acts and the severity of an individual child's problems with fire. These and other group differences remained significant at one-year follow-up. Looking longer term, a ten-year follow-up study by Lambie *et al.* (2013) measured the repeat firesetting behaviour of children and teenagers who received fire safety education from the New Zealand Fire Service (NZFS) following deliberately set fires. Of the 182 children followed up that had been referred to the NZFS Fire Awareness and Intervention Programme (FAIP), only 2 per cent were known for further arson offences (yet the overall rate of general offending for these young people was 59 per cent).

In the absence of a UK evidence base, this gradually accumulating body of research from elsewhere in the industrialised world has been my grounds for using fire safety education approaches in my direct work with children, teenagers and their families over the last 16 years. In the absence of best practice models in the UK, looking to the literature available elsewhere about what works enables me to be as effective, ethical and evidence-based as possible in my approaches. Does this compensate for what I consider to be a shameful – arguably negligent – gap in UK evidence and service provision? Absolutely not. Especially when these gaps were first brought to the attention of central government nearly fifteen years ago, in a document called the *Evaluation of Interventions with Arsonists and Young Firesetters* (Palmer, Caulfield and Hollin 2005). However, whilst these identified absences remain unaddressed by those bodies with the influence and budgets to do so, my work will remain rooted in fire safety education until someone tells me otherwise (and has the robust evidence to prove their counter argument).

Understanding child development

Given my use of research from outside the UK, it is important to consider whether findings from across different continents can generalise into other countries' populations and practices. We cannot know the definitive answer to this until the UK starts to build its own evidence, but in the meantime there is comfort in the knowledge that children's basic needs are fairly universal wherever they live and whatever their ability, accent, nationality, skin colour or religion. Children everywhere require protection, nutrition and stimulation. Put another way, they need love, food and play, particularly in the first three years of their brain development. Thus, as we start to consider the wider needs of children, it becomes apparent that our understanding of child development must be woven into the very fabric of our fire safety work and the educational approaches we deliver.

It is fair to say that for every champion of a particular child development theory there is an equally ardent critic. As such, the approach I propose here is most definitely open to critique and questioning – whenever we consider adopting different ways of working I see it as an ethical duty for practitioners to apply rigorous inquiry to the new ideas and information being presented – but in the absence of any national guidelines on how to deliver fire safety education messages to children and teenagers in a child-centred, age-appropriate way, this is the model I have developed in order to best ensure my work is rooted in theoretical foundations.

Russian psychologist Lev Vygotsky stressed the importance of play for children's development and as a path to the learning process. Play is considered the most authentic, truest creativity (Vygotsky 1926) and many of the techniques you will see used in Chapters 5 to 7 encourage play and being playful, be it with toddlers or teenagers. Whilst we may consider play to be the domain of younger children only, play at all ages encourages creative thinking and the solving of problems, skills that are no less important for adolescents to master. Vygotsky was a contemporary of the Swiss psychologist Jean Piaget, who proposed that as human beings we progress through childhood and adolescence in stages; a continuous process with a predictable sequence. In his work, Piaget (1936) identified four distinct stages of development in children's thinking and it is the application of his theory that allows me to evidence a theoretical underpinning in the decisions I take about what fire safety messages to use with children and teenagers. (For those children and teenagers whose development is adversely impacted by, for example, disability or trauma, Chapter 8 will consider how best we work with families where there are further, different needs to consider.)

Piaget's four stages of thinking development are:

1. Sensorimotor: birth to 2 years – children know the world through their movements and sensations and **learn about the world through their senses.**
2. Preoperational: ages 2 to 7 – children begin to learn to use words and pictures to represent objects; and while they are getting better with language and thinking, they still tend to **think about things in very concrete terms.**
3. Concrete operational: ages 7 to 11 – children are becoming

much more logical but **can still be very concrete and literal in their thinking, continuing to struggle with abstract and hypothetical concepts.**

4. Formal operational: ages 12 and up – teenagers have increasing logic and ability to understand abstract ideas, are capable of seeing multiple potential solutions to problems and are **able to think more scientifically about the world around them. They can also now begin to reason about what might be, as well as what is.**

What is crucial for fire safety work is not the names of each of these four stages but the age ranges within each group and *what we can reasonably expect children and teenagers to be able to understand* (highlighted in bold above). This has allowed me to develop the following model of practice:

Age of Child	Fire Safety Message for Child
0–7 years	*Stay away from fire* (combining Piaget's first two stages of development and reflecting children's very concrete thinking)
8–11 years	*Good versus bad fires* (reflecting children's literal thinking)
12+	*Fire science and the ability to consider 'what if' scenarios* (reflecting teenagers' ability to think more scientifically and hypothetically)

In linking fire safety messages to Piaget's theory of what a child can understand by which stage in their development, I ensure that my very youngest referrals (0–7 years) have a simple rule that they can follow – to stay away from fire. The next stage (8–11 years) are enabled to understand this rule by learning the difference between good and bad fires. At 12 years upwards, children are encouraged to explore and debate the logic and reasoning behind the rule in order to help them buy in to the idea.

As to buy-in, just as Piaget teaches us that children are not merely passive recipients of knowledge but constantly investigating as they build their understanding of how the world works, so you must also 'investigate' the use of my framework. Are there other accepted and respected child development theories that better serve you in delivering interventions that 'work' or can the application of Piaget's theory allow you to buy in to my recommended structure of three broad, over-arching fire safety messages at three key stages in children's thinking development? Ultimately, as practitioners we must evidence how we deliver in practice the emerging research findings which highlight that education-based approaches tailored to the young person's age and developmental level are important (Lambie, Seymour and Popaduk 2012). In my professional judgement Piaget's theory allows me to do this.

The use of shock and scare tactics

On a final note about what works, we need to spend a moment considering what *does not work* because – despite decades of evidence – there are still some practitioners that think the use of shock and scare tactics in our work with children and young people is okay. I could spend pages exploring and evidencing the reasons why it is far from okay but here are my top five reasons:

1. These approaches are largely ineffective (Kolko and Vernberg 2017).
2. Shock approaches can make behaviour worse (Haynes *et al.* 2012).
3. There is a marked difference between having a short-term

impact (shock effect) and the skills that practitioners require to bring about long-term, sustained behaviour change.

4. There is frequent stigmatisation of disabled people by the use of these messages. (How many shock ads over the years have featured people who use wheelchairs or those that are burned and scarred from fireworks?)

5. The 'forbidden fruit' syndrome of using shock tactics with teenagers is likely to be ineffectual. (Tell them not to do something and they'll do it all the more.)

But if you are still in doubt about the ethics or efficacy of the use of shock and scare tactics, then it should need no more explanation than this:

The use of shock or scare tactics has the potential to traumatise or re-traumatise children and teenagers.

As safe, trusted adults who are passionately committed to providing child-centred care and determined to do what works, we're better than that, aren't we?

CHAPTER 5

Working with Children Aged 0–7 Years

The previous chapter established that for this age group the key fire safety message is '*stay away!*' because for children this young their main motivation will be curiosity as they learn through play about the world around them. The youngest referral I am aware of for a child-set fire is an 18-month-old toddler who had taken a lighter and ran it back and forth along the floor, causing it to spark and set a fire. When you're 18 months old and see something in reach that is small, colourful, light and plastic with 'wheels' (the striking mechanism), it may as well be saying 'play with me'. It's as irresistible as the bottle saying 'drink me' to Alice in her adventures in Wonderland (Lewis Carroll 1865).

A fire caused by an 18-month-old immediately raises the question 'Who needs the fire safety education in this family? The child or their parents?' In this case it is clearly the parents and carers who need fire safety advice. Without this child being able to access that lighter, there would have been no fire; we're back to Professor Kolko and his insistence that removing accessibility to fire-lighting materials will automatically reduce juvenile firesetting. Arguably, whatever the age of the child or teenager, the more a parent can model good fire safety then the easier it becomes for children to be fire safe as they mimic the behaviours of others around them – 'monkey see, monkey do' as it were, a phrase which means to copy an action without actually understanding the reason or process behind it. (Whenever I use the phrase 'monkey see, monkey do' when training practitioners outside of Wales, it *always* raises a warm smile; I think it has something to do with my Welsh valleys accent.)

However, despite the vital role of parents and carers in modelling fire safety messages, Piaget's child development theory – as seen in Chapter 4 – teaches us that children build their own thought systems and will think differently to adults; after all, did we *always* do what our parents told us to do when we were little? Of course not. Therefore, this means that despite the everyday reality that many parents and carers will continue to leave lighters and matches accessible to curious minds even after a fire, very young children can still learn to *stay away* through the fire safety messages we teach them. How? Through the medium of play and being playful.

The easiest way I have found to teach children to *stay away* from matches and lighters is through the game 'Yes, I can play! NO! STAY AWAY!'. I created this simple game during my work with 4-year-old Aariz and his 5-year-old sister Safrana, who had set a fire at home by placing pieces of paper onto the cooker, turning the ring on and walking away. No intent to cause harm, no desire to burn anything, just simply copying what they had seen nan do: put things on the cooker, turn the ring on and walk away. During my first home visit with both children we completed a jigsaw together, coloured in and read the children's fire safety story book *Frances the Firefly* (all explained in more detail later in this chapter). Despite the children happily taking part in every activity and loving the story of curious Frances and the insect kingdom, my reflections on my first home visit troubled me.

Regardless of the book being suitable to their age, I had no confidence that the children would be able to connect their actions to the fire safety messages I had read to them. How could they? Frances sets a fire using a match yet these children were playing with a cooker. How can a 4- and 5-year-old understand that a story about a match means 'don't touch the cooker'? They can't. Not won't but can't. It's too sophisticated an application of one context to another meaning for a 4- and 5-year-old brain. I needed something that would simply teach these children to stay away from the cooker. And so the game was born.

'Yes, I can play! NO! STAY AWAY!'

Create a series of A4 cards that each depict an item that is either safe or unsafe to play with. Good examples of safe and unsafe items that young children can easily recognise are:

Safe	Unsafe
Teddy bear	Lighter
LEGO™ bricks	Matches
Robot	Cooker
Sandcastle	Candle
Child's bicycle	Kettle
Dinosaur	Scissors
Ball	Knife

The more colourful each image is, the more appealing it will be to younger children. It is also a good idea to laminate the cards so that they can be easily wiped clean and will last longer.

In order to play the game, lay all the cards face down on the floor.

Working at the child's level

Whenever you're working with young children, your expectation should be to sit on the floor with them. It makes playing games much easier and also stops us from looking like big, scary people who are towering over them. If you are working in a home that is really busy and perhaps doesn't have much space for play, consider taking along a yoga mat for you and the child to sit on. Only you and they are allowed to sit on the yoga mat, which will help allow the child to feel that it is their special, safe space that they can come back to if they wander off.

Turn over a card and show it to the child, asking first what the item on the card is to ensure that they recognise it. Once the item is identified (help them if they don't know what it is) ask the question 'Can you play?' If it is an item they *cannot* play with, as you ask the question shake your head and use a tone of voice and facial expression that suggests you are unhappy. Even if the child is unsure of what the correct answer is at this early stage in the game, they will take their cues from your body language and will reply 'no' (albeit hesitantly if unsure). Respond by saying 'That's right! Well done. You *stay away*'. Crucially, the card is given to a parent or is kept by you, saying 'I'll have it/Dad has it because you must *stay away*'. Turn over another card, the above sequence continuing every time an item they *cannot* play with is revealed.

When a card shows an image that a child *can* play with, nod your head and change your tone of voice and facial expression to convey that you are happy as you ask the question 'Can you play?' Again, a hesitant child will take their cues from you and answer yes. Respond by saying 'That's right! Well done! *Yes, you can play!*' and give the card to the child. They will quickly learn from your body language and verbal praise the images they can and cannot play with. By the end of the game, the child will have a pile of cards of all the things they *can* play with, whilst all the things they *cannot* play with are safely with you or their carer. At the end of the game, count up how many cards the child has and congratulate them on how clever they are for getting all those questions right.

Due to the child succeeding at the game, the praise you have given them throughout the activity and its repetitive nature, they will want to play the game again and again and again. Toddlers especially delight in doing the same thing over and over again as it allows them to master new skills, and we all like doing things we're good at, right? Playing the game again and again allows children to learn very simply but very effectively the simplest of fire safety messages – stay away.

Putting play into practice

After playing this game repeatedly with Safrana and Aariz in our sessions, during my last visit we walked into the kitchen and I pointed to the cooker saying, 'What's this?' 'Cooker' whispered two small, quiet voices in unison. 'Can you play?' I asked. 'NO! Stay away!' came the confident, energetic reply shouted from both children.

It really is as straightforward as that. This game is beautiful in its simplicity. Like every resource I share in these pages it's easy to put together, cheap (you can draw the pictures or print out free images you find online) and most importantly does the job. One of the cutest moments in my work was when, after just three sessions together, a 5-year-old boy from North London would say 'NO! Stay away!' in a strong Welsh accent. Children really are the greatest imitators and this is what makes the game so very effective.

Back to basics

Before beginning any game like 'Yes, I can play! NO! STAY AWAY!' we need to start with the absolute basics. This means we're on the floor – or yoga mat – with our felt tip pens, crayons, coloured pencils, chalks and paper of different colours. Having a range like this will not only bring instant colour to a session but also provide a variety of textures that can give children different sensory experiences; the feel and look of a felt tip pen on white glossy paper is different to using chalk on black matt paper. Drawing free-style lets the child learn that it's okay to use their imagination and be creative with you. It really doesn't matter if you 'can't draw'. Most of us are able to outline a house, person, dog or cat that a young child will recognise. The most important thing is that you're entering into their world of play and imagination.

Colouring in

How do you start a conversation with a very young child about a fire they set? I've walked on this planet for over 40 years but if someone I didn't know asked me about something I'd done wrong, especially if I couldn't really remember all the details, I'm not sure I'd tell them. Would you? So why do we expect our little people to be any different? With this in mind, an easy way to steer the conversation towards fire is to introduce colouring sheets and dot-to-dots of fire engines and firefighter cartoon characters they recognise. En-

ter 'fire engines colouring pages' into any online search engine and a host of sites appear where pictures suitable for toddlers and above can be downloaded and printed off for free. Enter 'fire service websites colouring sheets' and links to websites from across the world will provide a wealth of colouring-in sheets. This, entitled 'She is a firefighter' (designed by my mother!) is a particular favourite of mine because representation matters, and girls and boys need to see that jobs are open to all genders.

Mind your language

On the subject of representation, it is important that we recognise many children won't have the word 'firefighter' in their vocabulary; they maybe won't have seen many female firefighters and the media often still reports on firemen, despite the job title of firefighter existing since the 1980s. If a very young child talks about a 'fireman' coming to their house, it's important we don't shut down their story by correcting them on their use of language immediately. Listen first to all that they have to say and later in the conversation explain, 'Do you know what the proper word for a fireman is? It's firefighter, because girls and boys do the job. Now you know the proper word, can you tell others about it, too?' Remember, language matters. Always.

As you colour in the pictures and complete dot-to-dots of the firefighters and fire engines with the child, gently enquire, 'Have you ever seen a fire engine?' Now that they are at ease with you, they are more likely to admit that a fire engine came to their house. Respond by asking, 'I wonder why a fire engine came to this house?' They may admit the fire, or you gently acknowledge, 'I know a fire engine came to this house because there was a fire. Fires can be scary and so I have a very important job to do. I have to make sure we never have a fire again. Can you help me with that?'

Explain that you are going to play or read together a very special game or book all about staying safe from fire. Through the easy and joyful activity of colouring in, you've entered the child's world, shown you are playful and allowed for a conversation about fire to be introduced in a gentle, safe way.

Asking for help

When we ask someone for their help, it conveys that we trust them and that we think they are capable. Toddlers love to help adults wherever they can and safe, age-appropriate responsibility encourages children of all ages about how to learn to make good choices (de Thierry 2015).

Using stories

Frances the Firefly

Working with children and teenagers often demands extraordinary levels of patience, but there is one area where I have a very low threshold of tolerance. It is with practitioners who complain about the children's fire safety book *Frances the Firefly* because it is 'old'. Yes, *Winnie the Pooh* (first published in 1926), *Miffy* (first published 1955) and *Paddington* (first published in 1958), 'kids today' hate them because they're so 'old'. What practitioners are really saying is that *they* as the adults are bored of the book because of the number of times *they've* had to read it. First, and most importantly, it's about the children's needs, not ours, and second, the book is timeless. Stories involving animals often stay current (hence the longevity of Pooh Bear, Miffy and Paddington) whilst the relevance of its fire safety message is as important today as it ever was.

Produced by central government and available to download and print for free[1] the book is aimed at 3- to 7-year-olds and tells the story of Frances, a firefly who wants to make her tail glow but can't because she is too young. Frances is tricked by another insect into using the flame from a match as a substitute for a glowing tail, with disastrous consequences when she burns her wings and drops the lit match onto the forest floor below. Practitioners can

---

1   www.gov.uk

make the colourful illustrations and story all the more interactive as they ask children to point out the immensely strong ants, count the spiders' webs and imagine what the bees' honey tastes like. Children are likely to spot things in the book that we adults have never considered before, which is why this children's book can never be boring. It also has another vital message to discuss with children about keeping safe because Frances goes into the forest with someone she knows but doesn't tell another adult. What an important conversation starter with children to help keep them safe from adults or other children who may want to hurt them.

Our skill as practitioners reading this book is to ensure we make it relevant to the child. If a child dismissively says they've already read the story at school, roll with this resistance. Explain that we need to read it again because there's been a/another fire and so we'll have to pay extra special attention to the story this time. If they have played with a lighter instead of matches, ask what Frances should do if it was a lighter and not a box of matches she was shown. Should she still go into the forest with a lighter and not tell someone? Don't let your familiarity with the story lead to contempt for what is a really important and lovely resource. Best of all, use it to link with activities and messages already learned. After playing 'Yes, I can play! NO! STAY AWAY!', read *Frances the Firefly* and see if the child shouts 'NO! Stay away!' when you ask them if Frances can play with the matches. If they say, 'NO! Stay away!' you know that they're remembering and relating the fire safety messages you're teaching them. Crackerjack.

Connections

It's amazing the connections children will make to the characters in *Frances the Firefly* without prompting. I read the book to three cousins aged 6 to 10 who had set a fire when playing together at home. It was never clear who actually set the fire but what mattered was that they were all present when it happened, and all needed to learn never to do it again. When seeing King Chrysalis in the book, a grand butterfly with brightly coloured wings and a brown face, the 10-year-old commented, 'King Chrysalis is Jamaican'. 'Do you know what, I think you could be right,' I replied. For this black British boy of Jamaican heritage, he'd connected to the colours of King Chrysalis.

Five-year-old Noah and 2-year-old Lana caused an extensive house fire by playing with a lighter. When Noah saw the blackened wings of Frances after the fire, he pointed to his sister and explained how she had 'black stuff' (soot deposits) all around her mouth after the fire and was coughing a lot. It was through this connection Noah made with Frances that I was able to realise just how lucky the children had been to escape alive from the fire they had set.

Oh No, GEORGE!

In the absence of children's books with a specific fire safety theme, we need to get creative with the children's books that are available and look for general messages that support our work. Examples of board books for very young children include *Maisy's Fire Engine* (Cousins 2009) and *Peppa Pig: The Fire Engine* (2010). Reading aloud to young children stimulates their imagination and expands their understanding of the world. In addition, these themed books work in the same way as colouring in pictures of fire engines: they allow us to introduce the topic of fire in a safe way. However, there is one children's book that is especially perfect for adapting to a fire safety message and it just happens to be one of my most favourite children's books ever: *Oh No, GEORGE!*

Written and illustrated by Chris Haughton, *Oh No, GEORGE!* (2012) is about a dog called George who tries to be good but gets into all sorts of mischief when his owner, Harris, leaves him on his own. He just can't resist eating *all* the cake, chasing Cat and digging in soil. On his return, Harris is disappointed at the mess – and that George ate the *whole* cake – and George becomes sad that he had hoped to be good but wasn't. He apologises to Harris and gives him his favourite toy; Harris thanks George and suggests they go out for a nice walk together.

Time out or abandonment?

I couldn't love more that rather than sending George off alone after doing something wrong, Harris suggests he and George do something nice together. I'm a huge fan of 'time together' as opposed to time out. Time out is often suggested when a child's emotions or behaviour are appearing to become unmanageable, yet if time out is administered in the form of time alone, rather than providing a break from negative feelings, it can appear more like abandonment to the child or teenager. This will serve only to worsen the situation as it sends a message that children are on their own at a time when they need adults most in trying to cope with and understand their overwhelming feelings. Children need to feel connected to us to feel safe and so when setting limits on children's and teenagers' behaviour, we must stay connected emotionally and physically.

When out walking together, George sees *lots* of things he would like to do but passes a big cake, lovely soil and even Cat, without eating, digging or chasing anything. However, George eventually comes across something *very* interesting: a rubbish

bin. And there's nothing George likes more than rubbish. The book ends with the final question: 'What will George do? George?'

After asking a child what they think George will do next with the rubbish, ask what George should do if he found a lighter at home. Or a box of matches? What if he found a lighter in the park? Or a box of matches in the park? Then ask what *they* should do if they ever find a lighter or box of matches at home. Or in the park? What a clever, fun and safe way to have a conversation about lighters and matches. Chris Haughton has not only created a delightful and funny book, but a book that is also perfect for teaching children our main fire safety message of 'stay away'. Brilliant.

Jigsaws

As well as being fun to do, jigsaws help develop children's hand and eye co-ordination, encourage observation and help discussions. A range of high-street and online shops stock jigsaws of fire engines and firefighters, ranging in suitability for children from age 2 years upwards. As we saw with colouring-in sheets earlier, the use of fire engine jigsaws can help introduce the subject of fire in a gentle, non-confrontational way.

Like colouring and drawing, jigsaws can also help a child avoid having to make direct eye contact with an adult, which can help facilitate conversations that may feel frightening or shameful for the child to discuss. Whilst our eye contact is important for listening, observing and connecting better with a child, we must allow children the space and permission not to make eye contact with us, especially when a conversation is difficult or painful for them.

Songs

Singing songs with children has a huge impact on their language and communication development. Children especially enjoy listening to songs full of rhyme, rhythm and repetition, and so by singing fire safety songs containing these core elements we not only help boost their language, communication and literacy development but also teach them to stay away from fire in a way they can really enjoy and remember. Build in accompanying sign language, pictures and actions wherever possible to allow for even greater interaction and understanding.

The Never, Never Song (sung to the tune of 'Frère Jacques')

Never, never play with matches
If you do, if you do,
You might hurt your fingers, you might hurt your fingers
That won't do, that won't do.

Never, never play with lighters
If you do, if you do,
You might hurt your fingers, you might hurt your fingers
That won't do, that won't do.

Never, never play with candles
If you do, if you do,
You might hurt your fingers, you might hurt your fingers
That won't do, that won't do.

It is important that we are confident when singing songs as our sense of ease and enjoyment (or not) will be conveyed to the child. If we are having fun, then children are more likely to respond. As you sing, be confident. Sing slowly and clearly, consider using props, actions, widget symbols and pictures, and *encourage and involve the child.* The more they join in and enjoy the activity the less self-conscious you will feel.

Puppets

Puppets are engaging toys that can help support language skills and emotional development through safe, imaginative play. Most importantly, puppets can provide a sense of security that makes it easier for children to express their thoughts and feelings as they talk to, and through, a puppet. In Chapter 9 you will see how a sock puppet allowed 13-year-old Jenny-Lee to hear how worried I was about her. Working with puppets can help children and young people express their words and feelings more freely, allowing us to gain valuable insights into their life and what may have happened on the day of a fire, for example.

Six-year-old Julian had been repeatedly setting fires in his bedroom and was referred for support after a fire at home, attended by the fire service. A 6-year-old repeatedly setting fires raises huge concerns over a lack of supervision, boundaries and guidance, and basic care, and a call to social care confirmed a child protection social worker was allocated to the family. During my first home visit it was clear that Julian had very few toys to play with and so I decided that a puppet would be a useful prop during my second visit, used in a slightly different way.

To provide a more boundaried learning environment, all further visits to Julian were made at school, which also allowed me to check in regularly with the school about his wider welfare. As our session came to an end after 50 minutes spent colouring in, completing a jigsaw together and playing 'Yes, I can play! NO! STAY AWAY!', I explained to Julian that in my bag there was someone who had been listening to everything we had been doing. I asked if Julian would like to see who it was. Aged 6, Julian's world of make-believe and imagination allowed him to believe that somebody was indeed in my bag listening, and – like every other child of this age I've used this technique with – Julian couldn't wait to find out who it was.

Out of my bag I produced a dragon finger puppet and placed it on my finger. Stroking her head and tail I explained she's a very special, safe dragon because she doesn't breathe fire. When she wants to be angry she stamps her feet, meaning that she never breathes fire. As I told Julian more about the dragon (where she lives, what she likes to eat, her favourite place), I pretended that she had something to say. Holding the dragon close to my ear, I nodded and smiled in agreement at what she was whispering to me. By this point, Julian was enthralled. What *was* the dragon saying? I explained that, like me, the dragon thought Julian had done very well. 'She liked how you coloured in, really enjoyed the jigsaw and thought you played the game brilliantly. She thinks that you definitely deserve a sticker when we finish today. She also says that one day she would like to come and live with you but she can only do this when she is sure there are no more fires at home. Until I am sure there are no more fires at home, she's going to go back in my bag. When I am sure there are no more fires at home, she will come and live with you forever.'

Through the use of a finger puppet I had praised Julian for all his work in the session and also set up a reason to stop setting fires at home: to have his very own dragon. Needless to say, Julian asked about the dragon at the beginning of every session, sitting with her on his finger as he coloured, read *Frances the Firefly* and played 'Yes, I can play! NO! STAY AWAY!'. At the end of every session, Julian was awarded a sticker for his work and on our last meeting together one very proud 6-year-old left with a tiny dragon all of his own in his pocket. Dragons really are the stuff of magic (and can be found in the puppet variety at children's toy shops and online).

Stickers

In a world where technology develops and changes daily, nothing heartens me more than the sheer joy a paper sticker still brings to a child: that visible, lasting display that they have done well and you are proud of them. It's fabulous stuff. There is no shortage of stickers available on the high street and online, but a personal favourite of mine is the online family-run company the Sticker Factory. With a fabulous range of images, plus stickers in Welsh and Spanish, they also have a series of accompanying notepads.

If I've seen a child at school, the notepads are a quick and easy way to write a message to their parent, telling them how well their child did in the session. Whatever else may not have gone well at school that day, they can arrive home with a note from me that tells their parent or carer about the good things they achieved.

Rewards

Stickers are just one example of the importance of praise and rewards as reinforcing the behaviours we want to see. The way we respond immediately after a child's behaviour makes that behaviour more or less likely to happen again. If we want a child to be fire safe we must praise and reward this behaviour as it is more likely to happen again if it is followed by a positive consequence, like a reward. There are many different ways we can reward children and teenagers, and Appendix I contains a helpful list taken from Kolko and Vernberg's 2017 *Assessment and Intervention with Children and Adolescents Who Misuse Fire.* What I love most about this list is that every item on there is free because they are social rewards, not material ones. No money is required to give positive feedback and approval to a child. Affection (hugs and kisses from a parent, a smile from a practitioner), praise (including the words 'thank you') and 'attention activities' (an extra story read aloud for a young child, playing a game with a teenager) are some of the most powerful rewards. Perhaps the best things in life really are free.

Talking about emotions

Whilst receiving a sticker is likely to evoke feelings of pride and pleasure, it is also important to give children space for other, less positive feelings. In their 1991 paper entitled 'Family talk about feeling states and children's later understanding of others' emotions', Dunn, Brown and Beardsall cited four separate studies that provided evidence whereby from around the age of 20 months children are using emotive descriptions in their daily interactions with family members. Between the ages of 24 and 36 months, a 'dramatic increase' in children's vocabulary of emotional terms is seen.

For toddlers, the board book *How Do I Feel?* (2018) lets children turn the wheel to reveal how a new character on every page is feeling. Exploring five emotions that include scared, sad and angry, can link nicely when reading *Frances the Firefly*; for example, explaining how Frances was sad because she couldn't make her tail glow and became scared when the fire spread through the forest. Learning that it is okay to talk about emotions with you, a safe space is provided where a child can say how they felt before, during or after a fire.

Colour Me Happy! (written by Shen Roddie and illustrated by Ben Cort) uses colours to explore a wider range of feelings such as boredom and jealousy. I particularly like this book because it has the added texture of glitter on every page, allowing for an enhanced sensory experience. With a tiger in a tutu and a monkey eating ice cream, this book's gentle exploration of different emotions encourages children to talk about their own feelings. And we all know it's good to talk.

CHAPTER 6

Working with Children Aged 8–11 Years

We established in Chapter 4 that children have now reached a stage of development where they can think more logically and not just intuitively. Therefore, our main fire safety message with this age group is the difference between good and bad fires, with a heavy emphasis still on the importance of learning through play and having fun. At any age children will be more willing to engage in learning if it is enjoyable, and we all remember better if the process was more memorable because it was fun.

I cannot stress enough that *all* the activities suitable for working with younger children can and should still be used with this older age group. Colouring, jigsaws, puppets, *Frances the Firefly,* emotions, stickers and rewards remain absolute staples in order for children to continue learning through play. *Crucially, simpler activities and board books may still be appropriate for children whose thinking or emotional development is younger than their chronological age.* There is absolutely no expectation for children to 'act their age', but there must be complete acceptance on our part that we will adapt to whatever their learning and emotional needs are.

Card games

The principles of safe and unsafe objects that underpin 'Yes, I can play! NO! STAY AWAY!' can now be developed into more sophisticated games. Use the same images as in 'NO! STAY AWAY' but this time produced in card size to create a deck of playing cards. Double up the images of the safe and unsafe objects so that games like 'Pairs' and 'Snap!' can be played. If a child correctly matches an unsafe pair of objects, you will keep the cards to reinforce the messages that these are not items to be played with. Items like matches and lighters, knives and saws are never toys to play with but are tools that have important jobs around the home and garden. Whilst playing 'Snap!' and 'Pairs' together, keep emphasising the message of 'good versus bad' things to play with whenever an unsafe item appears on a card.

Good Fires, Bad Fires

Reading with children remains an important feature in our work for this age group and turns can be taken in reading aloud if the child is comfortable and able to do this. If not, give them the job of turning the pages and remember to ask them to point out different objects in the illustrations to help feed their imagination and allow them to become as active and involved in the story as possible.

The children's fire safety book *Good Fires, Bad Fires* was commissioned by the education department of Western Australia for use across the country. Written by Mary Flahavin and illustrated by Michael Salmon, it was published as a big book in 1981 and over 30 years later its message about the difference between good fires (barbecues, candles on a birthday cake) and bad fires (playing with matches) remain relevant to this age group. Contact with the Australian fire services and Michael Salmon has confirmed that there is no current copyright on the book, and Michael is particularly keen for the book to still be used wherever it can be helpful in keeping children safe. A PDF of the book to download and print for free is available.[1]

---

1   www.dfes.wa.gov.au/schooleducation/teachersandschools/JuniorTeachers
     Guide/Good_Fires_Bad_Fires.pdf

Children of this age group enjoy the large, colourful illustrations of this big book as they learn what happens to Olivia and her black cat. At the end of the story, encourage children to think of other good and bad fires, and how even good fires can become bad if we are not careful. Reading this book encourages children to think about countries elsewhere in the world, whilst

any book written over 30 years ago that shows a mum in charge of the barbecue and a dad tidying up will always win my vote.

Jez's Lucky Day

Jez's Lucky Day (Oddy and Strudwick 1999) is an utterly fabulous children's fire safety book.[2] Admittedly it holds a very special place in my heart because it is set in the South Wales Valleys – and the fictional town of Aberglyn looks exactly like where I was brought up – but its appeal to children is universal. I remember being particularly stunned when an education manager within an English fire service asked me what relevance a book set in Wales has for English children; I wondered if they would have questioned the relevance for English children of the stories of Heidi (Swiss), Tom Sawyer and Huckleberry Finn (American), Lola of *Big Hair, Don't Care* (Swain-Bates 2013; African-American) and Dora the Explorer (Latina). Having worked in London since the age of 24 I have mostly used this book in England and it is adored by children of every background and nationality, for who couldn't be transfixed by a story with a dragon and a hamster at its heart?

---

2   Originally published by Caerphilly County Borough Council in association with the South Wales Fire Service.

This beautiful big book, written by Michelle Oddy and Kate Strudwick and illustrated by Jason Hodges, tells the story of Jez, a boy who wants to make his cardboard dragon breathe fire. From the opening pages the wonderfully intricate and detailed pictures draw young readers in as you ask children to discover details like where the town's fire station and school are, how many children in Jez's art class have brown hair and which of Jez's classmates uses a wheelchair. Best of all, from page six onwards in the book a hamster becomes visible and children adore skipping back to previous pages to find him, giggling at his future exploits, which include eating chocolate biscuits and drawing a self-portrait. Crucially, the hamster becomes frightened when Jez lights a match, allowing us to explore with children their feelings about fire. At this point in the story it is useful to ask children to name the bravest animal they can think of. The usual answers of tigers, lions and dinosaurs can be greeted with the statement that even brave tigers, lions and dinosaurs are frightened of fire and naturally run away from danger. Explain to children in this upper age group (10 to 11 years) that it was an asteroid – a great big ball of fire – crashing into earth that killed off nearly all the dinosaurs 66 million years ago. This definitely shows just how dangerous fire can be.

In addition to the central message of never playing with fire, the book allows for many other fire safety conversations. The pages set in the family kitchen show a range of hazards not only for Jez but also his baby sister and the adults in the home, such as toys on the floor, matches placed on a shelf in easy reach of children and a tea towel hanging over the cooker hob.

Jez's bedroom also has dangers such as an overloaded plug socket, and when the fire starts he hides under the bed.

This provides a perfect opportunity to teach children about the correct thing to do when a fire starts, including escape plans, how to call 999 and the importance of working smoke alarms. With its accompanying teacher's notes that provide extensive prompts for discussions on language, literacy, fire safety and Welsh valleys culture, it becomes obvious how the book provides for several meaningful, enjoyable sessions, which enable children to learn the dangers of fire and a host of positive fire safety messages. At the end of the book, consider asking the child to be Jez and write a letter to a friend about what happened on the night of the fire, including how he felt afterwards. The possibilities of this book are endless – limited only by a lack of our adult imagination – making this book from Wales highly relevant to children wherever they live.[3]

Fire safety word searches and crosswords

I am a big fan of using fire safety word searches with this age group, especially as many children who struggle with language and reading will still be able to complete them and feel a sense of accomplishment as they finish the activity. Word searches also allow children to learn the importance of perseverance as they realise that staying with a task can get it done. A range of fire safety word searches can be found online along with websites where you can design your own, allowing you to tailor the words to the exact safety messages you'd like to teach a child.

The use of fire safety crosswords can be similarly effective and enjoyable. As well as a fun way to help children practise their vocabulary and problem-solving skills, the fire-related clues

---

3   For more information about Jez and how to purchase copies of the book in English or Welsh, email info@fabtic.co.uk

and answers can again enable discussions that teach a range of fire safety messages. As with word searches, a range of fire safety crosswords can be found online together with websites where you can design your own. There really is a wealth of free resources online that can help us in our work.

Hedgehogs, Hoses and Ladders

Another important part of play, board games help a child's thinking and social development as they find out new information presented in a different way and learn how to co-operate, such as taking turns and losing. Creating a new twist on 'Snakes and Ladders', it's all about the hoses and hedgehogs in a charming board game designed by Hampshire Fire and Rescue Service (south east England). As children climb the ladders and slide down hoses, they learn important road and fire safety messages – such as wearing seat belts and testing smoke alarms – in a fun and enjoyable way.

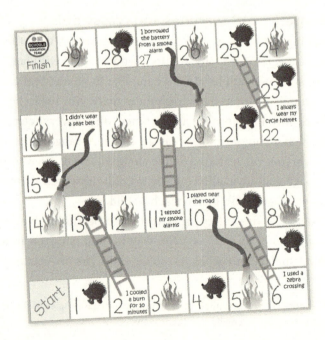

A version of the game can be found online, where you can print it out in colour.[4] Simply laminate, raid other games you have at home for a die and counters, and within minutes you have a shiny and colourful new resource to use.

Hampshire Fire and Rescue Service has also created a board game that is helpful when working with children who have limited understanding. With easy-to-follow footsteps on the board, children progress through the game using a die and counters to learn simple instructions like 'stop playing with matches'. The board also features question marks. Here you can create your own set of straightforward question cards tailored exactly to the child's abilities, and incorporating the specific fire safety messages you would like the child to learn.

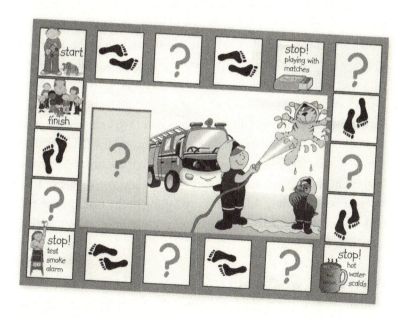

In addition to parents and carers knowing their children's learning needs, teachers and teaching assistants can be a huge help in

4   www.jkp.com/catalogue/book/ 9781785925337

guiding us about the level of a child's understanding – so when in doubt, ask. Or just ask anyway. It would be a shame for a child to switch off from this gentle, playful game simply because we've pitched the questions at a level that is too difficult for them to understand. When a child gets a question right, move along the board two spaces; if they get an answer wrong, move them along one space as a reward for trying.

A version of the game can be found online where you can print out the game in colour.[5] As with 'Hoses, Hedgehogs and Ladders', once this game is printed and laminated, find a die and counters and this game is ready to go.

Hazard house

An online search of the words 'hazard house fire safety' brings up a range of colourful cartoon images of living rooms and kitchens with different hazards to print out and use with a child. Spotting the fire safety hazards helps develop a child's concentration, thinking and attention to detail. This is because at first glance the room looks safe but as children look more closely they'll begin to spot the dangers. From clothes left on heaters to unattended pans on cookers, talk together about the pictures and the dangers they find. If a child struggles to find the objects that are unsafe, provide helpful hints and encouragement so that they don't start to lose interest because they think they are failing at the task. Praise the child for every hazard they find, checking out their understanding as to why it's unsafe.

What's hot, what's not?

Similar to 'Yes, I can play! NO! STAY AWAY!' in its theme of safe and unsafe objects, take an A4 piece of paper and draw on it the outline of items children can and can't play with. Good examples are matches, lighters, candles and kettles alongside crayons, balls,

---

5   www.jkp.com/catalogue/book/ 9781785925337

teddy bears and jigsaw pieces (notice that these are all things that are relatively easy to draw as a basic outline). As the child colours in the objects, ask them, 'What's hot, what's not?' As they correctly identify each item, praise their knowledge and stress the importance of never playing with anything that is hot.

If this game appears to be repeating the themes of earlier activities, it absolutely is. Whenever we learn essential skills for the first time it is all about practice. Repetition increases confidence and provides the practice children need to master new skills. Notice also the use of rhyme – yes, I can play, no stay away; what's hot, what's not. This again is deliberate. Many cultures around the world use nursery rhymes to soothe, entertain and teach young children because simple, repetitive, rhyming and rhythmic structures help babies and children (and adults) remember and retain words.

Creating a fire safety club

Asking a child to create their own fire safety club is a wonderful way to let them explore their imagination and consider different fire safety messages that can easily fill more than one session. Ask a child to imagine they are setting up their very own fire safety club. In creating their club, ask them to consider the following:

1. The name of the club.
2. Who is in charge?
3. The rules of the club.
4. The logo of the club and its strapline fire safety message.
5. Who is allowed to join? Is anyone excluded from joining?
6. Does the club have a uniform?
7. What dates and times will the club meet?
8. Where does the club meet?
9. What food and drinks are provided at the meetings?
10. Is there a fee to join the club?
11. What happens to members who break the club's rules?
12. Design your club's logo and motto.

The constant thread of fire safety through this activity is obvious, but the real beauty is the setting of the rules. Every time I've done this exercise the child has included a rule about not playing with fire; not only are children less likely to break rules they have set, it also shows us that fire safety is becoming important to them. Various parts of the activity can be expanded, for example, by asking the child to design a poster to advertise the club and to draw the club logo. This can be done together in your session or they can complete it by the next time they see you.

Another huge benefit to this activity is the tremendous insight it can give us into children's worlds. I'm always struck by the number of children from abusive homes that set 'no fighting or bullying' as rules for their club, yet their sanctions for anyone breaking the rules are often very harsh physical punishments. They are copying the aggressive behaviours they see in adults.

A world of pure imagination

It is really important throughout this activity to accept all the child's ideas, whether spoken or written down. It is *their* club and we have asked for their thoughts, therefore we mustn't shut down their voice or imagination by imposing our ideas on them. If they have said or written something that causes us concern, accept their ideas but explore the possibility of other ideas, too. For example, if their consequences for breaking rules appear excessively harsh, ask in what other ways we can respond to behaviours we don't like. We are still accepting of their ideas but planting seeds about other possible ways to be.

My favourite example of not shutting down a child's imagination was when doing this activity with 9-year-old Bobby and his stepfather. When Bobby was asked what uniform his club would have, he immediately replied, 'All the boys must wear red dresses.' Stepdad looked at me expectantly, seeming to want me to correct Bobby and say that boys don't wear dresses.

My reply? 'Red dresses. Okay. Are they dresses to the knee or to the floor?' 'To the floor.' 'And with short sleeves or long?' 'Long.' By this stage Stepdad had turned his own shade of red at the conversation that was unfolding. The activity continued and I left the session wondering what Stepdad would say to Bobby about his choice of clothing. During my next session with Bobby we read a copy of *William's Doll* (Zolotow 1972) – the children's story of a boy called William who wants to play with a doll but his father won't let him. I needed to make sure that Bobby knew it was okay for boys to like 'girlie' things. Whatever 'girlie' means.

From their choice of uniform to where they'd like to meet, from the food they will eat to who's in charge, this activity lets you learn so much about your child as they happily create, colour and imagine their very own fire safety club. It's truly wonderful stuff.

Singing

Singing can be a solitary activity but is often very social and communal, therefore the use of songs in our fire safety work can be one-to-one with a child or shared with their siblings and parents or carers as a way to encourage everyone to become involved in a home visit. Just like colouring, jigsaws and story books, fire safety songs can be another way of gently introducing the topic of fire.

There Is a Match (sung to the English folk tune 'Come Landlord Fill the Flowing Bowl'[6])

There is a match I will not touch
To always keep me safe-oh [repeat]
M-A-T-C-H

---

6   https://www.youtube.com/watch?v=cnvsoDGB7og

M-A-T-C-H
M-A-T-C-H
And always keep me safe-oh.

When you repeat the song for a second time, when spelling the word M-A-T-C-H the letter M is replaced with a clap of the hands. For example:

There is a match I will not touch
To always keep me safe-oh [repeat]
(CLAP HANDS)-A-T-C-H
(CLAP HANDS)-A-T-C-H
(CLAP HANDS)-A-T-C-H
And always keep me safe-oh.

When you sing the song the third time, when spelling the word M-A-T-C-H the letters M *and* A are replaced with a clap of the hands. This pattern is repeated every time, which means by the time you have sung the song five times all the letters are replaced by a hand clap when spelling out M-A-T-C-H. When singing the song for the sixth and final time, all the letters of the word M-A-T-C-H are reintroduced and sung (i.e. you don't clap any more). When reaching the end of the song, give the child (and any other family members who have taken part) a big round of applause for all the noise and effort they have made.

Fire safety skills

In addition to never playing with fire, children can learn lots of other skills to help keep them safe from fire. These include:

Testing smoke alarms

Advice on how often to test a smoke alarm varies across fire services, with suggestions ranging from weekly to monthly. I usually ask children in this age group to tell me their favourite television programme and what day of the week it's on. Let's imagine it's *The Simpsons* that's on every weekday. I explain that I want them to do a very important job for me; every Monday evening as soon as the music finishes at the end of *The Simpsons* it's their job to tell whoever's the tallest person in the house to test the smoke alarm. If you are a practitioner working with a child and family at home, during your home visit test all the smoke alarms with the child and their parents/carers. Make sure that children (and parents) agree and know what to do if they hear the smoke alarm. Walking around the home to check smoke alarms is a good way to expend physical energy, especially for those children who find it harder to sit still for prolonged periods.

Escape plans

Just as it's important for children to practise escape plans at school, it's as vital to practise escape plans at home. Whilst every home is different in style, size and layout, children will often share the same common misconceptions about how to escape from a fire wherever they live: many of them want to go out of the window. Ask a child how they usually leave their home when going to school and they will realise that the best route out in a fire is often the usual way in and out of their home. Develop and practise an escape plan with children and families during your home visits, with a plan for a second route in case the first one is blocked. This can be an especially fun and physical activity for a child as you encourage them to shout 'FIRE! FIRE!' as loud as they can. At an age when children are often told to be quiet, many relish the opportunity and permission from an adult to be as loud as possible.

If you are working with a child at school, ask them to describe their house to you. Use their descriptions to draw out a plan of their house, marking on it where the smoke alarms are fitted and planning all the different ways to escape, depending on where the fire is. Whether you are making and practising your escape plans in the child's home or school, there are lots of simple rhyming sentences that can help children remember your advice:

Get out, stay out.
Crawl under the smoke so you don't choke.
Get down low and go, go, go!

Introduce these short rhymes into your explanations and write them on any drawings of an escape plan the child makes.

How to call 999

Always check that children know the number to ring for the fire, police and ambulance services. In the UK it is 999 (but calls will still connect to an emergency services operator if you dial 911, the US emergency number). Role play with a child how to make an emergency call, with you as the operator, to prepare them for the information they will have to give. Do children know their full address? Repeat the role play until they, and you, are confident in making the call. Praise their work in achieving this new skill and stress that they must never make a 999 call as a joke (either on their own or with friends).

Stop, drop and roll

Stop, drop and roll is the technique used when clothing catches fire. Teach and practise with children the following sequence:

1. Stop where you are.
2. Drop to the ground and cover your eyes and mouth with your hands.
3. Roll over and over and back and forth until the flames are out.

It is really important that children know when to stop, drop and roll. They may have heard the phrase before, remembered it and mistakenly think that they stop, drop and roll when there is a fire (as one boy who'd listened to a school talk on fire safety told me). Emphasise that stop, drop and roll is only used when clothes we are wearing are on fire.

The Fire Safety Officer

As your work with a child nears completion because they are becoming fire safe, consider appointing them the 'Fire Safety Officer' in their home. Entrusting them with this very special job sends a message to them about how important and clever you think they are, and it is not unusual to see children physically grow in front of you because of how tall they are standing with pride. Furthermore, de Thierry (2015) teaches us that safe responsibility that allows a child to make good choices helps build resilience.

Tell them you would like them to become a Fire Safety Officer because of all their hard work and everything they have learned; say aloud *everything* they have learned so they can hear all that they've achieved. In addition to a sticker to praise them for this new job, make a firefighter helmet for them to wear. You can buy children's plastic firefighter helmets but mindful of both cost and how much plastic ends up as rubbish that is killing our oceans, I prefer to make mine from paper. Making the helmet with the child provides a nice shared activity in the session and will help build their sense of ownership and involvement in the job you have given them. Don't worry that the helmet won't be an exact fit as this models for the child the important message that things do not have to be perfect to be fun.

Make a firefighter's helmet

To make a firefighter's helmet you will need:

- a paper plate
- yellow paint

- paper and felt tip pens
- glue
- scissors
- elasticated thread.

1. First, let the child paint the paper plate yellow.
2. As it dries, take the piece of paper and draw a shield/ badge for the front of the helmet. Ask the child what words or letters they want to put on the shield. An example could be the child's name followed by the initials FRS (Fire and Rescue Service). Cut out the shield to use later.
3. Once the paper plate is dry make a U-shaped cut in the inner portion of the paper plate (size the cut to fit the child's head).
4. Glue the shield onto the inner flap portion of the plate and bend upwards to make the front of the helmet.
5. Use the scissors to make a small hole on opposite sides of the plate and pass through the elasticated thread, knotting the end.
6. Place the helmet on the child's head, secure the string under their chin and give a round of applause in celebration of them becoming a Fire Safety Officer. Explain that as the Fire Safety Officer it is now their job to ensure their home stays fire safe at all times.

Sparky® the fire dog

The National Fire Protection Association produces a range of brilliant fire safety activities that feature Sparky®, a Dalmatian fire dog. The full range of NFPA® Sparky® activities can be found online and three of my particular favourites are featured in

Appendix II.[7] 'Hot versus Not Hot' reinforces messages of good versus bad fires, the bookmark is a nice reward that can provide an ongoing reminder of your fire safety work once the session has ended, whilst as for the delight of seeing Sparky® come to life as you make an origami dog – well, when you create one you'll see it for yourself.[8]

Emotions

In this age group, as well as using the feelings of the characters in the fire safety books to explore their own – 'Olivia was sad after the fire, can you remember how you felt?' 'Jez was excited before the fire, what did you feel like before the fire at home?' – I also use emotions to instil a strong sense of positivity into our work from the very beginning. On first starting a session with a child of any age, I consider it my duty to find out as best I can how they are feeling (I use the word 'duty' because it's vital I avoid making a child who may be anxious, angry or scared feel worse).

I introduce the conversation by laying out a series of cartoon faces on the table or floor, depending on where we're sitting, that display a wide range of emotions. Examples of emotion cards and sheets can be found online to download for free. I explain that as a way of getting to know one another better, I am going to let them know how I feel about working together. I will choose the **happy** card, because I'm happy to meet them after hearing all about them from their mum and/or teacher; I choose another card that depicts a **sad** face, because I'm sad that there have been fires

---

7   www.sparky.org

8   These activities are reproduced with kind permission from the National Fire Protection Association, copyright © 2019, NFPA, Quincy, MA 02169. All rights reserved.

The name and figure of Sparky® are registered trademarks of the NFPA, Quincy, MA 02169.

at home and/or school; and the last card I choose shows a **proud** face, depicting how proud I will be of them when there are no more fires. I then ask them if they can tell me how they're feeling through choosing or pointing to the cards.

It's not unusual for children to copy exactly the emotions we have chosen; in their minds they can't possibly get the answer wrong or displease us if they are repeating what we've said. If they do copy exactly what you've said, acknowledge these answers by saying that you're glad they're happy to meet you too, that you will work your hardest to make sure there are no more fires that make them sad, and that you're very glad to know they'll feel proud when they become fire safe. If a different range of emotions is expressed, acknowledge and explore the feelings raised. For example, if a child expresses that they feel scared at what you might say, reassure them that you will never shout at them, and praise their bravery for still coming into the room even though they were frightened. By responding in this way a child will start to learn that it's okay to talk about emotions with you, whether those emotions are 'good' or 'bad'.

Did you notice how I was able to instil a sense of hope into this work from the very beginning, by saying I will be proud *when* there are no more fires (not if)? Feelings of hope and pride for the children and teenagers we work with are vital. If we don't feel hopeful and proud of them, how can they have any aspiration or pride in themselves? By taking the time to use emotions cards we send a powerful early message to a child that we really care about how they are feeling, are truly listening and are hopeful of the changes that can happen. Don't most of us respond better to people who make us feel cared for, listened to and allow us to believe that difference is possible?

Happiness is...

Twelve-year-old Benjamin loved to draw and we would begin every session by drawing our faces to show how we were both feeling. In our very final session together I drew my face with a big smile that showed all my teeth. I explained to Benjamin that I was very happy because there were no more fires, writing the words 'very happy' underneath my self-portrait. I asked Benjamin to draw his face, showing how he was feeling at becoming fire safe. Amongst a mass of curly hair he drew a big grin, underneath which were written the words 'even happier'. It remains to this day one of my favourite pictures.

CHAPTER 7

Working with Adolescents

Adolescence is the period when as humans we start to learn the skill of exploiting risk, because taking risks is an essential part of adult life. Growing up, risk-taking becomes an important part of mature reward-seeking as we gamble with the possibility of loss in the hope of making a greater gain (Bainbridge 2009). We can only make the journey safely from childhood, where things are mostly done for us, to adulthood (and the ability to take considered, informed and planned decisions) if we have been supported through this transition period and enabled to consider what are 'safe' and 'unsafe' risks. Therefore, a huge part of our work with teenagers who set fires is enabling them to see that the *disadvantages* of their risk-taking outweigh any possible advantages, especially in the long term. Ultimately, our fire safety work with this age group is looking to empower our young people in their decision making by allowing them to consider 'what if', 'what might be' and 'what could happen' when a fire is set.

Teenagers and the 'C' word
When I think about teenagers and inappropriate language, my 'C' word is the use of the word 'consequences' by adults. Using the word 'consequences' in discussions about fire with

children and young people usually makes me shudder, because it instantly sounds like a lecture from the know-it-all grown-up. You can almost hear the eyeball roll from the person receiving the 'advice'. Don't get me wrong; I absolutely agree that it is crucial for our teenagers to learn and discover the possibilities of what can happen as a result of the things they do – both for themselves and others – but it's about ensuring that these conversations are engaging our young people. We need to create a space for the young person's ideas and thoughts to be heard and provide an opportunity for them to reason themselves about the possible outcomes of their actions, as opposed to simply being told what to think, what to say, what to do and what not to do.

Playing games

In their 2017 practitioner guide, Kolko and Vernberg emphasise the importance of getting to know a child and teenager before we start discussing their firesetting. In addition to questions about who's important to them, their past experiences of working with services and their hobbies and interests, Kolko and Vernberg encourage the playing of games to help develop a positive and trusting environment. A pack of cards can be a helpful ice-breaker when working with teenagers, allowing you to get to know one another better in a more relaxed and fun way as you play together.

Notice the use of the words 'fun' and 'play' here. Adolescent work can conjure up images of the need for 'serious' conversations; but whilst these may need to happen, remaining playful in teenage work is as important as with younger children. The type of games will change as children get older, but enjoyment of play doesn't end in early childhood. Teenagers still like to have fun and laugh, especially as they learn. No matter how their play has evolved, taking the time to understand them and get involved inevitably leads to talking, connecting and building a trusting relationship.

Therefore, play remains as crucial for our teenagers as it does for our toddlers, especially if we are helping to model for parents something they haven't done for a long time; that is, have fun with their teenager and enjoy their company.

Tumbling tower/Jenga™

Standard versions of this game are readily available to buy on the high street and online, and some public libraries loan toys in their children's sections (yet another reason to love libraries). So, it may be worth visiting your local library to see if they have a version of the game that you can borrow. The standard game can be played in its own right for all the reasons of having fun and getting to know each other as described previously; but if you are able to buy a version that has numbered blocks, then the game serves as a way for targeted fire safety messages to be discussed and learned as the game is played.

Inspired by a technique used by the firesetter intervention team of Dorset & Wiltshire Fire and Rescue Service, my tumbling tower has 48 numbered blocks, which has allowed me to create 48 question cards. Numbers 1–24 are 'getting to know each other' questions and numbers 25–48 are fire safety questions. As a block is removed, the player is asked the question that corresponds with the number on the block. Appendix III provides an example of the questions I ask, but these can be tailored to the information you would like to know about, and share with, the young person you are working with. Given that everyone in the session is playing the game – remember to always encourage parents to join in if they are present – ensure that the questions about one another remain safe and appropriate; there are many things that a teenager and their families do not need (or want) to know about you.

Fire Safe Zone

Fire Safe Zone is a colourful and creative fire safety board game designed by social workers Karen Johnston and Robert Gitelson, and Doctor of Psychology Christine Krause.[1] For use by fire service staff, therapists and counsellors in their direct work with children and teenagers who set fires, this US board game can be played with a teenager individually, or their family can also be encouraged to get involved in the fun. Starting at a fire hydrant, players move along the colourful fire hose, responding to topic cards and earning chips along the way. The card categories include fire safety, decision making, win/lose, what's happening and 'go to the judge'. When a player reaches the fire station (called a 'fire house' in the USA) all the players count their chips and the player with the greatest number of chips wins.

In addition to covering fire safety, crucially the game encourages young people to talk about feelings, practise decision-making skills and make connections between their behaviour and what can happen next. Whilst in the USA the game is pitched as suitable for children from ages 6 to 12, I really like it as a game to play with teenagers. Using it at this age reflects the stages of cognitive development linked to fire safety messages I outlined in Chapter 4, and also the higher age of criminal responsibility in the UK when compared to the USA. (North Carolina has the lowest age of criminal responsibility at seven years, while Wisconsin has the highest at ten years. However, children as young as six have been prosecuted in those US states without a minimum age of criminal responsibility.)

The decision-making scenarios posed in the game are ideal for adolescents to debate and argue about what they would do in certain situations, allowing for rich conversations together as you play. There are some questions on the cards you may wish to avoid asking because they may not be relevant to your audience. One such example is the fire safety instructions given on how to use a fire extinguisher. In the UK, the advice given to children and teenagers is to never attempt to tackle a fire but to get out, stay out and call 999.

---

1   More information about the board game, including how to order copies, can be found at www.safetyzonellc.com

Apart from these geographical considerations, this US game happily transcends international borders and allows for meaningful conversations as you make your way together along the board.

Fire science

Games like Fire Safe Zone and quizzes such as those in Appendix IV frequently highlight that teenagers and their families are often mis-informed about fire because of images they see in the media. Fires frequently feature in soap operas and films yet rarely depict the realities of fire spread and smoke development because the story line is designed to entertain, not provide safety information. Therefore, it is important for teenagers to learn the realities of fire science and discussing the fire triangle is a good place to start.

The fire triangle

The fire triangle is a simple model that can help teenagers understand the necessary ingredients for most fires: heat, fuel and oxygen. Learning how a fire starts also teaches how to *stop* a fire from starting, for without these three elements a fire cannot happen. Many teenagers have studied the fire triangle at school but may struggle to remember the three elements. Help jog their memories by drawing out a triangle and the three elements as shown. Encourage a teenager to think about their bedroom and what can be fuel, what can cause heat and where the oxygen is (in the air). Your conversations will help a young person realise that virtually everything in their bedroom can be a source of fuel and their rooms will naturally be full of oxygen, so the biggest thing they can do to prevent a fire from starting is ensure that there is no heat source. Discussions about electrical safety – that lead into conversations about the need for working smoke alarms and escape plans, as learned in Chapter 6 – can be had. In this way we are helping to increase their levels of fire safety knowledge. Crucially, the very real danger of lighters and matches as a source of heat can be explored.

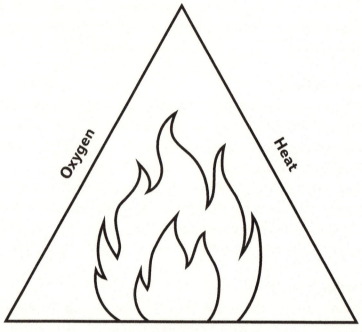

Fuel

Fire service advice and support

If you are a parent or practitioner, fire service websites can be a helpful source of fire safety advice and information. In addition, many fire services provide home visits where working smoke alarms are fitted for free and practical safety information tailored to a family's home and needs can be provided. Parents and practitioners can request this free service by contacting their local fire service headquarters or fire station in person, or via phone and website (see 'Organisations, Helplines and Websites Offering Support and Advice' at the end of this book).

Most fire services will also work with parents or practitioners where there are concerns for children setting fires. Working directly with the child or teenager at home or school, fire service personnel will teach a variety of fire safety messages, using ideas and strategies such as those in this book. Whilst Professor Kolko (2001) has evidenced that repeated fire safety education visits are more effective than a one-off intervention in reducing juvenile firesetting behaviour, it is not uncommon for some fire services to visit a child and family just once. Yet other fire services will work longer term to best address the firesetting concerns. This inconsistency in service sadly conjures up the phrase 'postcode lottery' and raises serious questions about the equality of support available across the UK to children and teenagers who are setting fires.

Fire development

To illustrate to teenagers and their parents or carers how quickly a fire can spread, I use photographic stills of a developing fire. These fire development photographs allow a teenager and their family to learn that within the time of an average TV advert break, a room in a house can be completely destroyed by fire. The photographs allow for useful and interesting information to be shared and explained, such as the four stages of fire – ignition, growth, fully developed and decay (burnout) – the poisons in smoke (including cyanide) and comparisons between fire and apples. Yes, apples, because fire is the same chemical reaction as when a cut apple turns brown or a nail turns rusty, a fact that surprises many people.

This process is called oxidation, where oxygen combines with another substance. Explain to your teenager that the difference between a fire and a discarded apple is of course speed; fire is an oxidation process that is so fast it produces light, heat and sound. The sudden release of energy can cause temperatures to rise by thousands of degrees and so we move our discussions from apples to pizzas. Ask your teenager if they eat pizza and if they know how hot an oven at home needs to be to cook a pizza. Most pizzas need to be cooked at 220 degrees centigrade, which a teenager is likely to agree is really hot. Yet a house fire can reach temperatures of 1000 degrees centigrade. That's really, really hot.

Through the fire development photographs, teenagers and their families have an opportunity to see how fire develops, the speed of its growth and the thick black smoke that can be produced. This enables teenagers to better understand what can really happen in a fire and also consider outcomes that they've not thought of previously. They can realise that 'fire is like a vandal' (the description given by a teenager who completed this activity with me) because of the damage it can cause *regardless of someone's original motivation.*

Fire science

Being able to describe accurately what happens in a fire is really important for the fire development exercise. If you do not feel confident having a conversation with young people about fire science and fire development, or are struggling to find appropriate fire development photographs online, ask your local fire service for help. If you are a firefighter or a fire service member of staff speaking to a teenager about fire development, remember to keep the information relevant and relatable. If you've started to talk about 'pyrolysis products and flammable by-products of incomplete combustion', chances are your teenager is possibly starting to feel a bit lost. I would be.

House of dreams

This resource was taught to me by the Early Intervention Education Co-ordinator at Hampshire Fire and Rescue Service. I love how in one simple exercise it allows for imagination, creativity, fire safety messages and, best of all, the relaxed conversations that can happen over cutting out.

For this exercise you will need a sheet of A4 or A3 paper, scissors, glue (or blu tac™) for sticking and an Argos™ catalogue; other catalogues are available but everything you could ever need for this exercise can be found in the 'laminated book of dreams' (as described by the comedian Bill Bailey). Explain to your teenager that they are going to create their 'house of dreams' and draw on the paper the outline of a three-storey house as shown overleaf. Invite the young person to fill and furnish their house using images they find and cut out from the catalogue. As in all the exercises where we ask young people to imagine and create their wishes, there is no right or wrong here. They can place a bath in the living room or a television in the toilet, it really doesn't matter. What's important is that they are being allowed to be imaginative, wishful and creative.

Once completed, be curious about what they've chosen and what it is that they like about the various items. Is there anything in their dream house that is in the house where they currently live? Their dream goods are likely to include electrical products and so you can start to discuss together where working smoke alarms should be fitted, which provide an early warning if an electrical item should overheat and catch fire. You can build on this discussion by considering other ways to keep safe from fire, such as escape plans and how to call 999.

For each room ask them to consider any potential fire safety hazards that are in their current home. For example, mobile phone chargers, laptops left on beds and hair straighteners (items owned by many teenagers) are common causes of house fires when left plugged in after use. Feel comfortable to work on your own dream house as the young person designs theirs. Taking part in an activity together can lead to a more relaxed, shared experience where the power balance that is usually in favour of the adults becomes more equal between us and the young person.

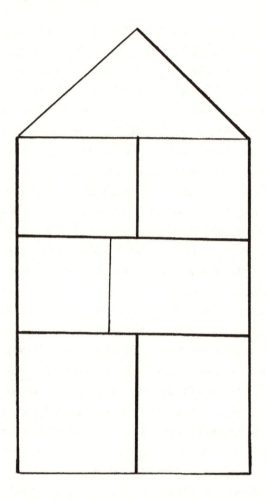

On learning about the idea of the dream house from the Hants FRS team, I was reminded of a question I was asked in my first week of working for the London Fire Brigade. My then Divisional Officer (a senior manager within the uniformed rank structure) asked me to think about the following question: 'If someone broke into your home, what could they take?' My answers included jewellery, TV and my cd player (it was a long time ago). My manager then asked me to think what could be taken if my home was on fire. 'Everything,'

I replied. It was a powerful realisation that could be as meaningful for a teenager. Gently ask them to think about what might be taken if someone breaks into a house. After listening to their ideas, explore what they think a fire in a house can 'take'. The purpose of this question is not to threaten a young person with what they could lose but to allow them to consider just how destructive fire can be, even if it was never somebody's intention. Reassure your young person that you will help them to learn how to keep safe from fire in their home now, which will help them stay safe in their dream home of the future.

The roll of a die

Adolescence can bring with it feelings of infallibility, omnipotence and invincibility, which empower teenagers to be the engines of energy and social change that every generation needs. At the time of writing it is our teenagers across the world who are taking strike action against climate change, not so much the adults. Yet it is this very same confidence in themselves that can cause some teenagers to dismiss the seriousness of firesetting, thinking that any worst-case scenarios won't happen to them. Indeed, they will often think it can't happen to them as they consider themselves to have control over the fires they set. Simply telling a risk-taking teenager that they may not be lucky in their actions has the danger of sounding like a lecture from the boring grown-up. Rather than inducing the inevitable eyeball roll, ask them to roll a die instead...

This activity involves some writing. We never want to deter someone from taking part simply because they may not be confident in their literacy skills, so ask the young person who they would prefer to do the writing. On a piece of paper, list the numbers 1 to 5. Ask the young person to think of five things that can happen if they set a fire and to write their answers against the numbers listed. Give encouragement where needed but try to let the young person create the list of scenarios wherever possible.

Usually teenagers are likely to think of realistic scenarios quite quickly and easily. Their answers are usually negative outcomes such as getting into trouble or getting burnt.

Once five things are written down, ask them to add number six to the list, which will be your idea. Your suggestion is that sometimes 'nothing happens' when they set a fire. (If they have already written 'nothing' or have identified a different positive reward on the list – for example, having fun – think of a different negative outcome as your idea.) Here is an example list:

1. Get burned.
2. Get into trouble.
3. Fire gets bigger.
4. Panic.
5. Run away.
6. Nothing happens.

Once the list is completed ask the young person to imagine they are thinking about setting a fire again. Using their list, ask them to choose which outcome they would ideally like to happen if they go ahead and set the fire they're thinking about. My experience is that they choose 'nothing happens' (or another positive outcome, such as getting attention) because they aren't usually setting fires to bring about worst-case scenarios.

Now pass the young person a die and ask them to roll the number that corresponds with the scenario they hope for. Even if they are successful the first couple of times when rolling the die, it just isn't statistically possible to always get the number they want. Thus, in a very visual and non-confrontational way this activity allows a young person to challenge their notion of being in control of what happens *after* setting a fire. A young person may be in control of the setting of a fire, but not what happens next. Ultimately, the greatest – and perhaps only – control they can guarantee is not setting fires in the first place.

When doing the roll of a die activity together it is important to use an actual die and not one on an app. A physical die allows for a more tactile, sensory experience as the young person sees, picks up, shakes and hears the dice roll. The avoidance of using an app also ensures that the boundary of no one using their phones in your sessions – including all the adults present – is not compromised. This is a boundary best set at the start of every session as it helps the young person to realise that you are there to listen to them without distraction.

Chewing gum for the eyes

In an episode of the comedy show *Father Ted,* Ted tells Dougal that TV is 'chewing gum for the eyes'. Child-like Dougal is glued to the TV, like so many of our children and young people who are seemingly transfixed by their screens (yet who are often mirroring the very behaviour of the adults around them). Whilst many fire safety activities can be found online on various fire service websites nationally and internationally, I always prefer to use resources children and teenagers can touch and feel, which require more social interaction between them and me.

Whilst I may need to modify this approach when working with a person who has autism for example, who may prefer to learn through screen activities that seem less intrusive and demand less eye contact with me, the likelihood is that most of our children's lives are already filled with screen time; it is quality adult time and meaningful conversations that are missing. Therefore pens, pencils, chalks, coloured paper and board games are as much a part of my repertoire in my teenage

> work as when working with younger children. We must give all our teenagers every permission and opportunity to be as creative and as imaginative as possible, for talent is evenly spread; it is opportunity that is not.

ABC

The ABC model is a familiar approach when seeking explanations for, and responses to, harmful behaviour. In a firesetting context it looks like this:

A – the **antecedent** (what happened immediately *before* the fire)
B – the **behaviour** (what actually happened *during* the fire)
C – the **consequence** (what happened immediately *after* the fire, including information about other people's responses and the eventual outcome for the person who set the fire).

As parents and practitioners it is really important for us to consider the before, during and after in order to help identify possible causes – and rewards – for the firesetting. As we ask a teenager these questions, our conversations can be helped along by using two different activities: dominoes and the graphing technique.

The domino effect

Ask the young person to think of a fire they set (their most recent or 'biggest' fire can often be the easiest for them to remember) and explore with them what happened before, during and after the fire. As they tell you, on a piece of paper write down all that they say under the headings 'before', 'during' and 'after' (ensuring they can see what you are writing). Once the lists are complete, gently read back everything you've written, checking that you've understood and captured correctly what they said, and if there is anything else they want to add. When the young person is satisfied with the account of the events, take a set of dominoes and for every individual thing that happened before, during and after the fire, a domino is placed standing up.

Am I bovvered, though?

As this activity requires a young person to talk about the fires they have personally set, they may be reluctant to discuss what they have done and refuse to take part, showing disinterest, rubbishing our efforts or even becoming abusive in the hope that their resistance will make us give up and go away. Reassure them that you are not there to tell them off but to help keep them safe. Remain patient and ask if they'd be prepared to see what the activity is like before they decide not to have a go.

Once you have lined up all the dominoes, get the young person to knock over the first one. All the dominoes will then fall over, allowing a visual representation of the knock-on effects of our actions. As you line up the dominoes for a second time, get the teenager to think again about all the events that happened before, during and after the fire. This time they have to identify which actions only *they* are responsible for (not what other people did or didn't do). When you have completed lining up all the dominoes, remove the ones that represent the actions they alone were responsible for. It is very likely that they will identify several actions for which they are responsible – including setting the fire – meaning a number of dominoes will now be removed.

With the relevant dominoes removed, now ask them to knock over the first domino again. This time, because of the gaps, all the dominoes won't fall down; the knock-on effect can't happen. This helps show our young people that by changing even just one of their actions they can prevent a sequence of events that they perhaps felt were almost inevitable or out of their control. On the contrary, they can indeed control what happens, which in itself is a powerful message for young people who are often powerless over the things done to them, for them and about them.

Note to parents and practitioners: Practise stacking the dominoes before doing this activity. This is so that you know exactly how far apart the dominoes need to be spaced so that when one is removed, the remainder of dominoes in the sequence no longer fall.

The graphing technique

The ABC approach is at the heart of the graphing technique that features in Kolko and Vernberg's 2017 practitioner guide entitled *Assessment and Intervention with Children and Adolescents Who Misuse Fire*. In addition to capturing the events of a fire, their use of the graphing technique also plots the teenager's changing thoughts and feelings before, during and after the fire. This enables young people to identify those situations, people, emotions and behaviours that are likely to result in them setting a fire. Kolko and Vernberg identified common factors leading up to firesetting as children being under-stimulated or left alone and arguing with parents or peers. The accompanying escalating feelings are frequently boredom, loneliness, anger and frustration.

Kolko and Vernberg suggest starting the graphing technique with the following questions about problem situations:

- You told me about things you like to do or are good at. Are there some things you don't like? What are they? Are there things you aren't good at? What are they?
- Do you ever find that things don't work out the way you want them to?
- Some of the children we see tell us that they sometimes don't get along with everyone. Is that ever true for you? How?
- What kinds of things bother you or get you into trouble?
- How would you like things in your life to be different?

Once the young person is at ease with doing the activity, describe to them that when something happens we have three reactions:

- One type of reaction is **feelings**. For example, if we get into a fight, we might be feeling angry, which might make our heart beat more quickly, our fists clench, or our stomach might get upset.
- The second type of reaction is **thinking**, which is what we tell ourselves. Like if we were angry, we might think, 'I am going to explode' or 'Why am I so stupid?'
- The third type of reaction is **behaviour**, that is, what people do to try and feel better, like yelling, throwing a toy or punching a wall.

Explain that you're now going to explore each of these reactions as you discuss their fire and/or what they burned.

(Taken from Assessment and Intervention with Children and Adolescents Who Misuse Fire*, Kolko and Vernberg 2017, p.47)*

Take a piece of paper and ask your young person to think of everything that happened before, during and after the fire, writing down their answers (ensuring they can always see what you are noting down). Ask if they remember what they were thinking or feeling at different points during the series of events. Write down the emotions and thoughts they experienced, asking them to grade the intensity of each thought and feeling from 0 to 10 (with 0 being the lowest intensity and 10 the highest). It helps if you have found out information about the fire they are discussing in advance, for example from a parent or member of an emergency service that may have attended, so that you can help prompt their memory. You could even begin by telling them what you already know about the fire, which may help them start talking about what happened if they are feeling anxious, ashamed or guilty about it. The following questions can help someone tell their story:

- Can you tell me what happened?
- What was happening to you before the fire? What were you doing?
- What were you involved with? What was going on at the time?
- What were you feeling (how did you feel) before the fire?
- Did you feel anything else then? How else were you feeling?
- What were you feeling just after you set the fire?
- Did you have any other feelings after the fire?
- What happened after you set the fire?
- How did this end? What happened last?
- Did anyone notice the fire?
- How did others respond (later on) to the fire?

Once you have captured all the events and accompanying thoughts and feelings (with their grades of intensity), the information can be plotted out on a graph. The horizontal axis plots out events, and the vertical axis plots the thoughts and feelings on a scale from 0 to 10. Different shapes on the axis or the use of different coloured pens will be needed to differentiate between each emotion and thought. As you develop the graph:

- Review each detail carefully to verify correctness: (e.g. 'Is this right – let's see, this line shows how bored you were, this line shows how angry you were, and this line shows how sad you were.').
- Clarify how the child felt at the time and the impact of the fire (e.g. 'So you were really bored and had nothing to do, but you were only a little bit angry at your sister, right before you set the fire.').

- Ask if there are any more important details to the fire that the child can recall.
- The finished graph(s) should then be placed in the child's file.

(Taken from Assessment and Intervention with Children and Adolescents Who Misuse Fire, *Kolko and Vernberg 2017, p.51)*

In addition to helping a teenager learn about the three reactions of thoughts, feelings and actions, this activity allows both of you to better understand their reasons for setting fires and what the predictors and risks for further firesetting may be. If a young person talks about loneliness because of repeated periods of being left home alone, intense anger at a person or situation, or the desire for revenge and retaliation, this exercise can help identify the need for support beyond fire safety education alone. A referral to social care would need to be considered and/or support from child and adolescent mental health services (CAMHS) for an assessment of more specialist help to be considered. For example, your young person may benefit from CBT that can help with specific thought and behaviour responses and more pro-social reactions in stressful interactions (Kolko and Vernberg 2017).

See Appendix V for an example of a completed firesetting graph as provided by Kolko and Vernberg (2017).

In their practitioner guide, Kolko and Vernberg include the graphing technique as an example of a CBT exercise. By using it in this book and when using it in my fire safety education work, I am not playing at 'pop psychology' or blurring the boundaries of my role. Rather, I am using the technique as a way to allow for conversations that can help identify when I need to refer to other agencies for more specialist support. Just as we use our professional judgement to determine the number of sessions, content and activities a child or young person needs, so you will apply these same skills to determine how best to use the graphing technique.

The ripple effect

The ripple effect exercise is a very powerful and visual way to help young people start to explore, identify and begin to understand just how wide an effect fire can have on themselves and others. On a large sheet of paper (flipchart size works best) draw a series of circles around each other that start small and become gradually larger, like the ripples on a pond if you throw a stone into the water. Next, describe to your teenager a real-life fire that has happened. My preferred example is the M1 case study (see Appendix VI) because it is a fire involving ten young people where nobody was physically injured but there were many knock-on effects.

Once you have read together the details of the fire, ask the young person to consider:

- Who was affected by the fire?

Write down everyone the young person identifies as being affected and ask them to then think about:

- How were those identified affected by the fire?

Again, write down all the reasons given and provide encouragement and prompts where needed to help them expand their ideas.

Next, on a set of coloured sticky notes write out all the different people they identified. *It is important that every person is written on a separate note.* Now ask the young person to think about:

- Who was most affected?

They do this by placing the sticky notes on the ripples you have drawn out; those most affected will be in the centre. Using sticky notes allows the young person to easily move people about as they think more about how they were affected. Often, the young people accused of setting the fire are placed in the centre of the ripple, as can be seen in the exercise completed by 13-year-old David (see below). Whilst it is more usual for notes to be placed at random angles on the ripple shape, David placed his uniformly on the picture. This shows that there is absolutely no right or wrong to how a young person carries out the exercise; what matters is that they are starting to identify the impact that one fire can have. David and I did this exercise using a pool table to lean on. When we stepped back and looked at the image he had created, David softly said, 'It's thousands.' These two words show that David had realised just how vast the unintended outcomes can be when a fire is set.

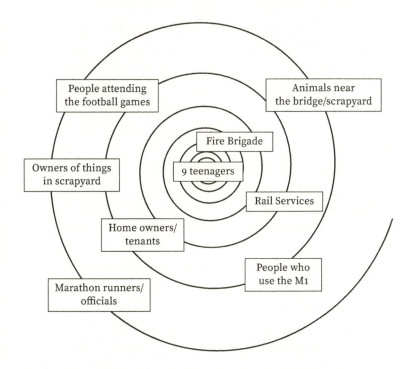

Emotions

The graphing technique nicely introduced safe ways to discuss feelings with young people, which is crucial for the emotional wellbeing of all our young women and men. If we are serious about wanting to improve people's mental health, and changing the fact that suicide is the biggest killer of men under the age of 45 in the UK, we mustn't let the negative stereotypes of grunting teenagers or misplaced beliefs that 'boys don't cry' get in the way of denying our young people the space and permission they need to express their feelings. Here, we put aside 21st-century technology and allow the humble felt tip pen and paper to provide adolescents with the tools to talk about their emotions.

The heart exercise

In Chapter 6 I explained how using emotion cards can instil a strong sense of positivity into our work from the very beginning. They can also help us find out how the young child we're sitting with is feeling. This is equally important with teenagers, but rather than using emotions cards I prefer to use paper, a range of coloured pens and an exercise that I learned during training with the children's charity Place2Be. Let's imagine it's the first time of meeting...

Introductions

As practitioners we must never take for granted that children (and their families) know – or remember – who we are, especially if professionals are constantly coming in and out of their lives like revolving doors. It's vital that whoever we are working with really understands who we are, the organisation we are from, why we are there and how long we will be there (both that day and overall). It sounds achingly obvious but in our busy working lives we can sometimes forget the fundamentals.

I also use my introduction to reassure a child or teenager about what I will and won't do, including who I might speak to if I am worried about their safety, that I will always take

---

seriously what they tell me and I will never shout at them, even if they have done something I don't like or don't agree with. You can sometimes see the tension ease away as the person hears you're never going to raise your voice or lose your temper with them.

After introducing myself I explain that I'd like to get to know the person a bit better, including how they are feeling about us meeting and working together. I go on to say that I will show them how I am feeling by doing what is called the heart exercise.

On a piece of paper I draw a heart. Taking a different colour felt tip pen, chalk or crayon, I colour in part of the heart and say that I am feeling **happy** about meeting together for the first time, especially after hearing so much about them from other people like their parents, teachers and social worker. Choosing a different coloured pen, I colour in a similar size section of the heart and say I am **worried**, because it always worries me to hear about fires being set. Finally, I take a different coloured pen and colour in the remaining (and largest) section of the heart, explaining that this represents my positive feelings. I say how I am feeling really **positive** about working together because I have done this work for a long time and most of the teenagers I work with become fire safe, and there is no reason why they should be any different.

If you're thinking the emotions I express sound very similar to the approach I used in Chapter 6, you're absolutely right. The fact I feel the same whether I work with a 6-year-old or 16-year-old doesn't mean I'm being disingenuous; it's simply reflecting my genuine feelings for my work. This is because it couldn't be truer that whenever I meet someone I'm always very happy they're there – it's really concerning when someone doesn't turn up – and of course I'm worried about them setting fires (or I'm in the wrong job!). I believe absolutely in the possibility of change so why shouldn't I be hopeful that they will be able to learn about how to become safer from fire?

When thinking about using the heart exercise, it is crucially important *not* to talk yourself out of doing this activity because you think young people, especially boys, will be put off by the use of a heart. Remember that by doing the exercise first, we are effectively saying to teenagers that it's okay to talk about these things and to work in a more creative way. As was said recently to me by a male firefighter, 'It's really powerful for boys to see men do this exercise.' I couldn't have put it better myself.

David's heart

Thirteen-year-old David (mentioned earlier in the chapter) was referred to me by his family support worker after his mother raised concerns for his firesetting. This included burning paper and plastic in his bedroom and creating a flame thrower in the garden with a friend, using an accelerant and a lighter. On first meeting David, I used the heart exercise to explain

how I felt about working together and meeting for the first time. I then asked him to do the same. David was curious (about what we were going to talk about), positive (because I'd said I wasn't going to shout at him) and confident (because he's always confident). I would always begin my sessions with David in this way and his final heart (shown above), completed in our last session together, captured his thankful, happy feelings that he 'got there'.

Joanna's magic onion

I learned this technique during restorative practice training delivered by Surrey County Council. By the end of the course it was nicknamed 'Joanna's magic onion' because of the magical effect people thought it had when I used it in a role-play activity. If we are to become more aware of the truly damaging impact of trauma (that is, to ensure we are 'trauma informed' in our work), we must recognise that children and teenagers hide vulnerability by acting angry or tough. This simple activity provides a young person with the opportunity to acknowledge and understand this.

On a piece of paper, draw an onion, as shown below, and explain that just like an onion has lots of layers of skin, we have lots of layers of feelings.

Choosing a fire, or another time where your teenager acted aggressively, suggest that it seems like in their outside layer – the one that everyone saw – there were feelings of anger. If they agree, write the word 'anger' in the outer layer of the onion. Then ask if there was another feeling they had that was underneath the anger. If they can identify another feeling, write this on the next layer, repeating this as many times as they are able to identify a different feeling.

However, they may struggle to do this as we often don't give our young people – especially boys – the words or permission to express feelings other than anger. If this is the case with the teenager you are working with, gently suggest that what often sits deep underneath people's feelings of anger and aggressive actions are really hidden feelings of fear. Write 'fear' in the very middle of the onion, asking if there is something that they are feeling scared about. If there isn't, that's okay; simply reassure them that if they are ever frightened or scared then they can tell you. However, it is quite possible that this is the first time they've been asked this question; that someone has taken the time to care and wonder what's happened to them, as opposed to what's wrong with them. This could be the first step towards a teenager realising it's okay to say what's going on. What's really going on.

CHAPTER 8

Adapting Our Work and Providing Additional Support

In Chapter 4 I outlined the need to align specific fire safety messages with certain ages. This is with the aim of being as ethical and effective as possible in the information we are providing to children and teenagers. Alongside the general approaches I recommended, there is an expectation that we will always make adaptations to our sessions, the messages we give and the resources we use in order to best meet the needs of our clients. This consideration applies whether it is a child, a teenager or their parents and carers. We are truly child and family focused when our usual ways of working are changed without fuss, in order to best reflect the person sitting in front of us in that very moment.

Given that this can include adapting to the child with attachment disorder, the father who requires an interpreter, and the teenager that needs support beyond fire safety education, this chapter has a broader focus than 'special educational needs and disabilities' (SEND) and 'social emotional and mental health difficulties'. These two definitions from the Ministry of Education (2015) include learning difficulties, learning disabilities and 'underlying mental health difficulties such as anxiety or depression, self-harming, substance misuse, eating disorders or physical symptoms that are medically unexplained…[and]…disorders such as attention deficit disorder, attention deficit hyperactive disorder or attachment disorder' (p.98).

Acknowledging the army of people that have dedicated their entire working and academic lives to understanding each of these areas, and out of respect to the many thousands more that are affected daily by living with these diagnoses, to attempt to summarise each of them here would be insulting at best and potentially damaging at worst. For, to paraphrase Dr Stephen Shore, if you've met one person with anxiety/attachment disorder/autism/ substance misuse/eating disorders/mental health difficulties, you've met one person with anxiety/attachment disorder/autism/ substance misuse/eating disorders/mental health difficulties.

Vive la difference

Dr Stephen Shore is a professor at Adelphi University, New York, where his research focuses on matching best practice to the needs of people with autism. Non-verbal until the age of 4, as a child Dr Shore was diagnosed with 'Atypical Development and strong autistic tendencies' and was deemed to be 'too sick' for outpatient treatment. He famously said, 'If you've met one person with autism, you've met one person with autism', highlighting that whilst the commonalities of people on the autism spectrum can include differences in communication, social interaction, sensory sensitivity and highly focused interests, there is also great diversity within the autism spectrum. This diversity and variability from child to child and adult to adult applies to every single one of us, whatever our diagnosis.

Examples of child-focused work

Reflecting on the reality that we are all different, the most useful contribution I can give on adapting our work to meet individual needs is to tell you about the times when I've had to take different approaches. Some examples may surprise you as they may not fit with our usual image of 'additional needs' but each aims to highlight exactly what child-focused work looks like. As with all the case studies in this book, identifying features have been changed to respect the privacy of the families I work with but the scenarios described have not been exaggerated.

Michael

Seven-year-old Michael set a fire whilst playing with an incense stick. Michael was diagnosed with attention deficit hyperactivity disorder (ADHD), autism and attachment disorder, which suggested he would need a repeated, predictable routine and that I most definitely needed to understand how best he learned. Therefore, I always visited him on the same day of the week and at the same time in school, in the presence of his teaching assistant Ms Bradley (whereas I will usually see children on my own). Ms Bradley was a familiar, safe constant for Michael who could allow for trust to be felt in the room from our very first meeting together. Ms Bradley also guided me in how Michael learned best, which included him being able to keep his hands occupied as he listened. To help channel Michael's physical energy in a safe and productive way as he listened, I brought a set of building blocks to each session, which he could play with as we chatted together. Although Michael couldn't follow the instructions on how to build the blocks into the 'proper' shape of the fire engine, he merrily fitted the shapes together and by the end of the session he always created at least one version of a recognisable fire engine. Did it matter that the other times he made a vehicle that was unrecognisable as a fire engine? Of course not.

It was not unusual for Michael to hide under the table at the start of every session and so I would tell him that Ms Bradley and I would be colouring in at the table and that he could join us whenever he wanted to. Like most children and teenagers, Michael found it hard to resist being left out and would soon join us in the colouring in. Patiently waiting and colouring, as opposed to demanding he sat 'properly' on a chair, gave Michael the time he needed to come out from his hiding space. Despite appearing to enjoy colouring, building and reading stories, after every activity Michael would ask, 'Can I go back to class now?' This was consistently met with a calm, reassuring '*When* you hear the school bell ring, *then* you can go back to class', a repeated, clear instruction that allowed him to continue with the session. Ms Bradley was given a copy of *Frances the Firefly* (see Chapter 5) to read in literacy sessions with Michael, which provided further repetition of the 'stay away' fire safety rule he was learning. We were confident progress was being made when Granddad told me that whilst out for dinner as a family, Michael had told the waitress that she had to 'stay away' from the lit candle on the table. The waitress duly blew out the candle.

Christopher

Eight-year-old Christopher had been setting fires since the age of 4. He is diagnosed with ADHD and often became easily distracted in our work together. When wanting him to do something very specific, I would always begin an instruction with his name. For example, 'Christopher, please put the pencils in the box'. Saying his name first meant it was more likely he would hear the instruction first time. This simple modification allowed Christopher to learn that he could indeed stay on task and get things done, of which he became very proud. We built on this success to the point where at the end of my long-term intervention (that had taken place alongside support from his child protection social worker and music therapist), Christopher was appointed the class fire safety officer with the responsibility of sharing with his classmates the fire safety messages he had learned over our 11 sessions together.

Lucy

Ten-year-old Lucy denied setting a fire in her bedroom, explaining that her younger brother had done it. Lucy and her brother are adopted and she is diagnosed with attachment disorder. Despite her social worker confirming Lucy and her brother had never been abroad either before or after their adoption, Lucy would often talk to me about the alligators she had seen when she visited America. Just like adults, children lie. Children who have experienced trauma (which is to be expected with any child or teenager who has been removed from their birth parents) will often lie because real life is just too scary and horrible to talk about. Also, we know that memory is affected when someone is traumatised (de Thierry 2017) and so perhaps Lucy really couldn't remember setting the fire. If I simply considered her a liar and insisted she told me the truth, I could cause further trauma and make it highly unlikely that she'd want to see me again. Instead, I listened to her truth and we explored together the difference between good and bad fires without ever needing to insist that she had indeed set the bedroom fire.

P-J

Eleven-year-old P-J was referred by his social worker for fire-setting behaviour. Both his CAMHS worker and mother told me that I could try to visit him but there was no way he would ever stay to talk to me or engage in any of my work. Arriving at the family home and sitting on the settee waiting for P-J to come into the room, I could hear him making his way down the stairs and heading out the front door, throwing a cursory glance my way as he left. About 20 minutes later he came back to the house and sat next to me on the settee. We started chatting and stayed speaking together for the remainder of my visit. Before leaving and agreeing my next visit date, I asked what had made him come back. His answer? When you first saw me you smiled at me.

Maya

Twelve-year-old Maya had been setting fire to paper and other items in her bedroom, which she had done on and off for as long as she could remember. Maya has attachment disorder and learning difficulties, and we would always meet together at her SEND school because of the structured routine this provided. Maya wanted our final session to be at home so that her aunt could hear all that she had learned.

It sounds achingly obvious but being punctual with children and families really matters – it's respectful, shows we care and that we do what we say. I had never been late for a meeting with Maya but for my final session I was delayed because of a broken-down train. Hailing a cab I arrived about 20 minutes late. Maya, who had always seemed very happy to see me, was furious. Absolutely furious. She was screaming at her aunt about how useless I was and that she didn't want to see me. Through the kitchen door I told Maya how sorry I was. And I was. I genuinely was. It was our last session together and I really wanted her aunt to see all that she had achieved, how proud I was of all her fire safety work and for Maya to experience a safe ending to a positive attachment she had formed. Thinking I had lost her for good during this final meeting, I told her exactly why I was late and how I'd even flagged down a black cab to get there from south to west London. After a silence that seemed to last forever, Maya opened the kitchen door and stormed past me, muttering under her breath that she still didn't want to see me. Yet rather than heading for the front door or her bedroom, she flung herself into a chair in the living room. For all her resistance, she did indeed want to be there. And so did I.

Ricky

Thirteen-year-old Ricky had been setting grass fires close to the area he lived in. Identified as having learning disabilities, Ricky attended a SEND school. Despite his chronological age, we worked to his developmental level that was estimated to be about 9 to 10 years. Rather than the usual teenage approach of considering fire science and exploring 'what-if' scenarios, Ricky learned about the differences between good and bad fires through the activities discussed in Chapter 6. He especially loved playing board games. During one home visit, his younger sister complained to me that he wouldn't get his hair cut and that she hated it because he looked like a girl. Given that Ricky generally responded well to my suggestions, I think she was hoping I would tell him to get his hair cut. Instead, I said that I thought it looked nice and suited him.

Three years after I had finished working with Ricky, his family support worker contacted me and invited me to attend an award ceremony for Ricky, which celebrated his completion of an education course he had attended. Already grinning widely at seeing Ricky again and learning how well he was doing, my grin widened further when I noticed he still had long hair.

Desmond

Fourteen-year-old Desmond set fire to a local school. Desmond has learning disabilities, attends a pupil referral unit (an educational provision specifically for children who have been permanently excluded from school), is diagnosed with oppositional defiant disorder and had been displaying sexually harmful behaviour towards a younger child at school. He was also hiding weapons for a local gang and had previously attacked a rival gang member with a cricket bat. In our sessions together, Desmond found it much easier to talk if he was drawing free-style. Once absorbed into his drawing he would chat freely, which allowed for a safe space to be created where we could learn and explore together the difference between good and bad fires. Beneath the externalising violence was a frightened and vulnerable 14-year-old boy who needed a safe place to play and learn like the young child he still was developmentally.

Em

Fifteen-year-old Em was referred by his youth offending team officer for setting fire to cars in his local area. Approximately halfway through our first home visit whilst chatting together, Em 'exploded' in temper with no suggestion or change in body language that he was starting to get angry or upset. Slamming every door along the way, he returned to his bedroom and within seconds the Manic Street Preacher song, 'Stay Beautiful' started blasting from behind the door. In case you are unfamiliar with the song and think it could be interpreted as a compliment to my looks or a respectful nod to my Welsh origins, the chorus includes words that say 'I don't want to see your face, I don't want to hear your words and why don't you just...' (the original song included the words 'fuck off' but this was later replaced with a guitar fill). Message received and understood, Em. I stayed in the living room chatting to Em's grandfather for the remainder of the time I said I would be there and before leaving slid a note under his door saying sorry I'd upset him and that I hope we'd get on better next time.

Curious and concerned about what could have led to such an unexpected loss of temper I asked his social worker if she was aware of anything that I hadn't been told that could explain what had happened. One of the saddest life stories I have ever heard in 16 years of practice unfolded. Em was living in a constant world of fight or flight due to dangers that had been real and were now imagined because of severe and chronic early abuse and neglect. In that moment, Em was unable to contain inside this heightened state of absolute terror any longer and so 'exploded'. Knowing this, when meeting Em for the second time I again apologised that he had become so upset and that this was never my intention. He shrugged, stayed for the remainder of the meeting and attended all further sessions. I still can't listen to that song without thinking of him and hoping he's okay.

Tina

Sixteen-year-old Tina was referred by CAMHS after setting a fire at school. CAMHS are working with Tina as she has social anxiety and bulimia. Despite agreeing to meet at home for the first time, Tina was too anxious to meet with me and wasn't at home when I arrived as agreed. Upon learning about how nervous she was about meeting, I wrote a short letter to her explaining very simply who I was and why I'd like us to meet. Tina attended the next and all future sessions with me.

She is one of many teenagers I have written to when they've not turned up as originally planned, like Peter. Whilst I was on the phone to his mother to introduce myself and my work to her and her family, 15-year-old Peter asked his mum who she was speaking to. Upon hearing it was a woman from the fire service, Peter responded, 'Tell her I ain't fucking seeing her.' Despite my numerous letters and visits, I never did meet Peter but perhaps by getting my letters he still received the message that somebody cared.

Rob

Seventeen-year-old Rob was referred by his social worker for support and advice on safe smoking habits. Rob has autism and this case was unusual for me to work with because he was not setting fires. However, his social worker had identified the potential fire risk in the home because Rob regularly smoked in bed. Over three home sessions I devised a set of fire safety house rules that Rob agreed to follow, which included clear instructions like 'Never smoke in bed' and 'Always use an ashtray'. Rob's mum placed the rules on the fridge so that they could be seen every day. Rob asked if I would write out a second copy of the rules as he wanted to put them on the wall in his bedroom next to his picture of the Queen. I think it's fair to say that Rob took his new set of fire safety rules very seriously indeed.

Working 9 to 5?

I usually visit children during weekdays and evenings but due to this particular family's working patterns this was not possible. The family also observed Shabbat (Sabbath), which in Judaism is a weekly day of rest observed from sundown on Friday until the appearance of three stars in the sky on Saturday night. Therefore, all my home visits were made on a Sunday.

Poverty

Eleven-year-old Daniel, 9-year-old Kyle and 8-year-old Jordan had worked really hard to become fire safe. Although Jordan had never set a fire, he was included in my work at home with his older siblings because my general fire safety messages were as relevant and useful to him. At the end of our work together, a trip to a fire station was the perfect reward to bring together all that they had learned and achieved as a family. However, the long bus journey from home to the fire station was costly for a family of four whose only source of income was Dad's disability allowances. A few phone calls later, a fire service mini-bus with a designated driver was arranged. Children growing up poor miss out enough on school trips; this family was not missing out on their trip to the fire station.

Guiding principles in all our work

Despite these families' different ages, abilities, histories and considerations, certain patterns can be seen that are transferrable into all our work:

1. We will often need to deliver our fire safety messages in ways that are younger than a child's chronological age.
2. The importance of a predictable routine and the use of clear, consistent structures – especially around fire safety rules – can be hugely helpful for children and adults with autism.
3. Longer-term intervention can start to build trust amongst children and teenagers who have experienced adults as frightening, abusive and unreliable. Longer-term work also allows for the repetition, reinforcement and practice of new information for children with learning disabilities and learning difficulties.
4. Persistence and patience from practitioners really are virtues, even when we're told to 'Just...'
5. Being curious about, and understanding, a child's 'bad behaviour' is not the same as promoting, advocating or normalising it.
6. Building blocks, stress balls and doodling can all provide safe, productive distractions for busy hands and minds that find it difficult to concentrate, or find it hard to make eye contact.

7. A grown-up saying sorry shows we care and that adults often get things wrong. By apologising we can help model for children and teenagers how relationships that 'break down' can be put back together.

8. Children's 'lies', 'deceitfulness' and 'manipulation' are often the coping mechanisms they develop to have their emotional needs met when adults have failed to keep them safe.

9. The damage caused to children and teenagers by bad relationships can be repaired by good relationships.

10. Government figures report that there are currently 3.7 million children living in absolute poverty in the UK (Department for Work and Pensions 2019). When children grow up poor they miss out – and so do our communities.

What is also very apparent in the cases presented here is that many children and teenagers who set fires face a range of complex difficulties, requiring support from several agencies and practitioners. A combination of interventions is often necessary to fully address their needs because fire safety education alone cannot provide the wide safety net that is needed to keep children and teenagers safe from harm.

Identifying appropriate support

We must also remember that firesetting poses a risk to other people, regardless of any intent. Therefore, as practitioners in this field we are constantly having to make decisions about the most appropriate level of support for behaviours that can potentially have fatal outcomes. In the absence of any standardised firesetter risk assessment tool available in the UK to non-clinical practitioners, I again turn to the guidance provided by Kolko and Vernberg (2017) for support in making evidence-informed decisions about the most appropriate form of intervention. Kolko and Vernberg's 'hierarchy of intervention components and strategies' considers six different areas that can make up a continuum of care for children and teenagers who set fires:

1. Consideration of the environmental exposure to fire (i.e. the firesetting can 'disappear' as soon as a child's access to lighters and other ignition sources is removed).
2. Providing fire safety and skills (i.e. fire safety education).
3. Teaching behavioural skills, such as pro-social modelling, problem solving and safe coping strategies when angry or anxious.
4. Addressing parenting and family problems, for example through parenting programmes and family therapy.
5. The involvement of youth justice, for example the use of restorative justice.
6. The removal of a child or teenager from home to prevent the risk of further harm to themselves and/or others, for example a child placed into therapeutic foster care.

By reflecting on this six-stage intervention hierarchy, I start to consider the most appropriate response for the children and teenagers referred to me for firesetting behaviour. I can absolutely address numbers one and two, often working alone unless there is other agency involvement because of wider child protection or welfare concerns. As we get to number three, this will act as my trigger to consider the very real likelihood that other resources and people are needed to best meet the needs of the child or young person. Realistically, some cases may already have other agency intervention at levels five and six – for example, a young person has been charged with the crime of arson or has been placed into care by the time they are referred to me – but the need for fire safety education can still be relevant and timely in the context of a wider support package that has been identified for the child or teenager.

Psychosocial intervention

Then there are of course those cases where I am not best qualified to support a child because they, and their families, are requiring help beyond fire safety education. This approach is described as 'psychosocial intervention', which would appear as numbers three and four in the Kolko and Vernberg hierarchy. These are the cases that require collaboration with, and most crucially input from, CAMHS, who can deliver the behavioural interventions that are able to target the individual and family needs that are influencing the firesetting behaviour (particularly around affect regulation and cognitive control). These are the children, teenagers and families that are suited to the modular behaviour intervention approaches that are outlined in Kolko and Vernberg's 2017 practitioner guide.

I would encourage all practitioners working in a CAMHS or other therapeutic setting to consider using the guide in their work with children and teenagers who are setting fires. The guide includes screening and assessment tools intended to supplement more general clinical assessment procedures that are typically used for treatment planning. It also incorporates clinical principles and techniques from several perspectives, including behavioural theory, family-system models and CBT. Through a series of activities designed for children, teenagers and their families, the guide promotes the expression of safe, pro-social behaviour by addressing the intrapersonal and interpersonal contexts within which the firesetting often occurs.

Knowledge is power

The fact I have made reference to CBT and 'intrapersonal and interpersonal contexts' is, by its very nature, suggesting we have moved beyond a world of fire safety education and therefore must refer to other sources of support to help best meet the needs of our children and young people. Yet this does not mean that any of us working in the field of teaching fire safety skills and knowledge are any less impactful in the continuum of care a child or teenager setting fire needs. Similarly, it does not mean that we have permission to be any less pro-social in our work because somehow our role and actions matter less. Whether we are the non-clinical practitioner reading *Jez's Lucky Day* with a child who has set their first fire, or are a psychologist delivering the UK's first and only standardised treatment programme for adult arsonists in prison (Firesetting Intervention Programme for Prisoners; Gannon *et al.* 2015), we each have knowledge and authority that can empower others, lessen risk and reduce harm. As the case studies in this book demonstrate, fire safety education has the power to be transformative long after we have finished our work with a child and young person. For that we should be deservedly proud.

CHAPTER 9

Working with Jenny-Lee

A Case Study

Background

I started working with 13-year-old Jenny-Lee (Jenny for short) when I was still manager of the London Fire Brigade's juvenile firesetter intervention scheme. Firefighters attended an emergency call made to Jenny's block of flats one weekday evening after a neighbour within the inner-city high-rise complex had seen her drop lit pieces of paper from her balcony onto the communal garden areas below. The neighbour called 999. When the firefighters called at Jenny's home nobody answered the door but the caretaker confirmed that the girl who lived there had 'an interest in fire'. (It later transpired that the police community support officer at Jenny's school knew about her firesetting and had nicknamed her the 'pyromaniac'.)

> **All behaviour is communication**
>
> Before we learn anything more about Jenny, as curious practitioners there are already questions that we can start to wonder from the limited information we have:
>
> 1. Jenny's flat was overlooked by hundreds of other flats in the block. Was she hoping someone would see what she was doing?

2. Why didn't anyone answer the door when the firefighters knocked? Is Jenny home alone?
3. If the caretaker knows she has an 'interest in fire', what's happened before? Has anyone worked with her and her family to address this?
4. What might Jenny be communicating through her firesetting?

Entering Jenny's address into the scheme database flagged up that she had been referred previously, after her mother had taken her to a local fire station for advice about her firesetting behaviour. During this visit to the fire station a firefighter spoke to Jenny about how quickly a house fire can spread and agreed with Mum to make a referral to the brigade's firesetter intervention scheme. Despite a series of telephone calls and letters from scheme staff to Mum, no further contact was had with the family until the second referral 11 months later. In our subsequent conversations, Mum explained that she hadn't accepted intervention because at the fire station a firefighter had spoken to Jenny about the dangers of fire. Jenny commented that the advice from the firefighter hadn't worked because she felt angry and humiliated at being taken to a fire station.

Being rigorous in our work

The second referral for Jenny led to a change in practice within the team I ran. Jenny's case had closed with no further action after the first referral due to a lack of contact from the family, yet on reflection what guarantees did we have that the firesetting was no longer happening? How could we be confident she was no longer at risk from potential harm through firesetting? If at the point of reaching case closure we had contacted social care (children and family services) for the area, they would have confirmed that Jenny had an allocated social worker who could have facilitated contact between us and the family. Yet as a scheme we didn't make this check. I hadn't made this check. I had authorised case closure without the due rigour this work demands. I reflected on Jenny's case as a 'near miss', for what if the second referral had been for a fire where she had hurt herself or someone else? From this point on I introduced the procedure whereby before taking any decision to close a case because of failed contact with a family, a routine check is made with social care to ensure we're not letting a child slip through a net of safety.

As the second referral raised the possibility of Jenny potentially being a child at home alone who was setting fires, I contacted social care, who confirmed a social worker was allocated to the family. The newly allocated social worker agreed to my first home visit as she was also concerned about the firesetting, which Jenny had described to her as having an 'urge' and 'overwhelming feeling' to do.

First home visit

Jenny lived at home with Mum and her black cat Merlin. From the first moment of meeting Jenny she appeared emotionally younger than her 13 years, playing an almost 'peek-a-boo' game as she peered and disappeared around the living room door before entering the room. When I asked about Jenny's likes and dislikes, she talked about enjoying school, with drama and science being particularly favourite subjects. (It was much, much later that Jenny admitted she hated school due to bullying from her peers, and these subjects were the 'better' ones because they had fewer bullies in the class. As Jenny began to trust me, she felt able to tell me what she really felt and thought in response to my questions.)

Thinking Jenny had an interest in science allowed me to lead into a conversation about fire science and I invited Jenny and her mother to take part in a fire safety quiz, which involved looking at a series of pictures of a fire developing in a room and guessing the correct timings for each image. (There was nothing that could be regarded as upsetting in these pictures; for example, they did not include any images of people or animals.) Both were willing to take part in the game, but as it progressed Jenny started to cry and went to her bedroom. I finished the fire safety exercise with Mum and knocked on Jenny's bedroom door. She invited me in and I was immediately struck by the contrast between the living room and her bedroom. Whereas the living room was comfortably furnished, Jenny's room was without carpet or curtains and smelled strongly of ammonia, which is recognisable as the smell associated with stale urine (I would go on to discover that Jenny was still wetting the bed). Jenny was sitting on her bed colouring in and I asked if I could join her.

With her permission we spent the remainder of the session colouring and chatting about subjects that ranged from school and crocheting (which Jenny enjoys) to the stars at night. During this time Jenny spoke about not feeling safe in her bedroom because of noises in her wardrobe. She also explained that she became upset during the fire development exercise because it had reminded her of the conversation she'd had with a firefighter at the fire station. She was also frightened at the thought of what could happen to Merlin (the cat) if there was a fire. I asked Jenny if she would be prepared to help me keep her and Merlin safe from fire, to which she happily agreed. She declared we would be the Firefighting JJ Club (JJ standing for Jenny and Joanna). We agreed that our next session would be at school, which is where I saw her at monthly intervals for the remainder of our 14 sessions together.

Pet power

Never underestimate the importance of pets in providing 'hooks' for changing firesetting behaviour in children and teenagers. Many children have very strong attachments to their pets – all the more so if their experience of adults is frightening or abusive – and are devastated at the thought of anything happening to them. The transformative and connecting power of animals stands out for me in two particular cases of mine – Jim the hamster and Ronnie the rabbit.

Jim belonged to 10-year-old Tamsin, who was so traumatised from sexual abuse by her mother that she would not speak. When I first saw Tamsin at home, because of fires she'd been setting in her bedroom, she made very little eye contact and spoke not one word. When I spotted her hamster cage in the corner of the room, I said how much I loved hamsters and I'd had a pet hamster named Shelley when I was Tamsin's age (true story). Still with no words, Tamsin suddenly came alive and animated. Within seconds the door of the cage was open and there was Jim the hamster in my lap. With his jet-black eyes and ever-curious whiskers he was easy to adore and Tamsin's love for him was obvious; still without making direct eye contact with me she watched my every move as I held her most precious thing. Jim provided the perfect introduction to *Jez's Lucky Day* (see Chapter 6) and Tamsin loved the story, finding the hamster on every page and pointing to the fire safety hazards when asked.

I saw Tamsin five more times after my first home visit, with sessions held at CAMHS, where we coloured, drew and read and re-read *Jez's Lucky Day*. With no further firesetting taking place, I explained to Tamsin at our penultimate session that the next time we worked together would be our last session. During this final session, after we had read the Jez story for the last time and I said goodbye, Tamsin looked at me and spoke the only word she ever said to me in all our meetings. She quietly said the word 'Jim'. I replied, 'Yes, Tamsin, Jim.'

As for Ronnie the rabbit, he was bought as a present by an uncle of three brothers I was working with, who were aged 13, 15 and 17. All three boys were setting fires and each had learning disabilities, which meant that their understanding of danger was far more limited than would be expected for teenagers of their ages. All three boys enjoyed setting fires and it was something that they were arguably 'good' at. By this I mean that their firesetting would often go undetected until they argued with one another and then one brother would tell their parents what the other had done. Despite all three being present whenever a fire was set, the boys considered the person who had set the fire as responsible, whilst the others were simply there (I am in awe to this day at the endless patience of this family with their children). Yet these three lively, risk-taking and hugely energetic dynamos were transformed into gentle, caring and calm boys who would do everything possible to ensure that Ronnie could never come to harm from fire. Ronnie was the hook that allowed the boys to understand why the number one rule at home was 'stay away' from fire.

Concerns beyond firesetting

Due to Jenny's fear of being in her bedroom and imagined noises in the wardrobe, the contrast between the conditions of her bedroom and the living room, the strong smell of ammonia that indicated long-term enuresis (bedwetting), and her firesetting, I left my first home visit deeply worried for the emotional and physical wellbeing of a young girl who I suspected was being hugely neglected. These concerns were shared by Jenny's social worker and school child protection officer, and between us we became an army that battled for her safety. Over the months that Jenny worked and chatted with her social worker, child protection officer and me, she disclosed – and we discovered – that neglect and physical and emotional abuse had been the hallmarks of her childhood for as long as she could recall (and even before she could remember).

Seeds of change

In conversations with Mum, the social worker and the school child protection officer, I was able to establish that Jenny's firesetting included setting alight newspapers, burning a kitchen work surface, melting plastic pegs, setting fire to a Bratz doll bought for her by her mother (which melted when set alight and burnt her hand) and setting a fire outside when encouraged to do so by other children who lived locally. Yet despite the extent of the firesetting, prior to our second session there were already early signs that Jenny was taking seriously my request for her help in keeping Merlin safe. On a home visit her social worker found Jenny busy designing and colouring a fire safety poster about protecting Merlin. Already I had enough clues as to what could be the potential hooks for bringing about a change to Jenny's firesetting – Merlin and allowing her to express herself creatively.

Session two

Our second session began with the heart exercise (see Chapter 7). Whilst I drew my heart, reflecting my emotions of worry (for Jenny's safety), pride (at knowing she had made a fire safety poster about Merlin) and excitement (at all the creative work we'd do together), Jenny drew a crocodile. If you haven't worked it out already, she is a brilliantly funny, inventive and clever girl. Around the crocodile she drew the words 'excited', 'jumpy' and 'adventurous'; excited because the day before she had laughed with girls at school, jumpy (which she explained was another word for excited) at being in the session, and adventurous like she wanted to explore a forest. When

I asked if laughing with girls at school didn't always happen, she began to cry as she explained that she often talks to herself using different voices, causing her peers to think she's 'weird' and to 'hate' her (Jenny's words). She went on to explain that she liked using voices because her 'childish brain' is nicer than her 'teenage brain' and the conversations that teenagers have. After being reassured she could use her childish brain as much as she wanted in our sessions, she drew a brain of two halves.

Whenever I work with a teenager, I always check with them if everything I've been told about their firesetting by other people is right, or if I have maybe made a mistake in what I know. As I started to do this with Jenny, after admitting to some of the fires she said that she didn't want to talk about it any more. When I asked why this was, Jenny answered, 'Because I like you.' It appeared that Jenny feared I would no longer like her if I knew she had done 'bad' things, so I assured her this wasn't the case; I simply wanted to know what had happened in order to help keep her as safe as possible. She confirmed that everything I had been told about her firesetting was correct, and we explored her ideas about what could happen when a fire is set. She spoke about the flames possibly spreading and potentially burning herself, commenting that she had previously burnt herself twice on melting plastic (not the once I knew about). I thanked her for her honesty and bravery in telling me about all the fires she had set, and we concluded the session by each doing the 'hand of hope' exercise:

Hand of hope
For this exercise, take a piece of paper and a pen and draw around your hand. In each digit, write a hope that you have. By doing the exercise first you can give a young person an insight into yourself; my hopes usually include areas like what I will

eat later, that I am always safe on my bicycle, that the young person and I will work well together, and that they will become fire safe. By going first, it can also help encourage a young person to have a go at what may traditionally be thought of as a 'childish' activity. Finding out what a young person hopes for can provide a crucial insight into what is important to them. It can also provide the opportunity for a fire safety conversation to develop. For example, if a young person talks about a job or travelling, are they aware that being caught setting fires could impact upon their future plans because some countries and jobs may not be open to people with an arson conviction?

The hand of hope exercise can be used in many different ways, including describing five (safe) things the person doesn't know about you, and five pieces of fire safety information learned in your work together. It is simply about having a creative conversation that relies on more than just the spoken word.

Jenny's hopes were to get good GSCE results, to have a great Christmas, have a gigantic cheesecake, to be a star and to be a billionaire. When I asked what would make a great Christmas, I was told it would be money for presents as currently there wasn't any. (It came to light much, much later that she was often home alone in the dark when Mum was at work because the electricity meter had run out, and setting fires was a way of feeling less scared.) My hopes for her were that she would be safe from fire, that Merlin would be safe from fire, that she would brush her teeth twice a day (poor dental hygiene had been raised as an ongoing health concern for her during a child protection meeting), for Jenny to sleep better (as she was now sleeping on the floor because of the extent of her bedwetting) and that we would share tangerines together, which I would bring to the next session.

Creating safe sensory experiences

Training I received at the Gestalt Centre, based on the work of child and adolescent therapist Violet Oaklander, stressed the importance of allowing neglected and abused children to connect with their senses through new, safe sensory experiences. Given the vivid orange of tangerine skin, their often cool, smooth feel, the strong, zingy smell as soon as they are peeled and the taste – will it be sharp or sweet? – I decided tangerines would allow Jenny to enjoy a positive sensory experience and the nurturing effect of sharing food. So began a routine of starting our sessions with a piece of fruit and a single Babybel™ cheese, whose red wrappers have the advantage of being used in collage work (explained in Chapter 10).

Signs of change

A week after our second session, Jenny told her social worker that she had been burning plastic pegs on her balcony but that this was okay because she had a bowl of water with her to put out the flames. This 'safety measure' was something she hadn't done before, but there was clearly much more for her to learn in our fire safety journey together.

Session three

Whilst eating our tangerines at the start of the third session, we checked in on one another's feelings by drawing self-portraits. Out of the mouth of Jenny's picture came the words 'excited', 'happy' and a 'little sad': excited and happy to be in the session and a little sad because of an argument in school the previous day where she had been accused of stealing, which had made her feel very angry. This allowed me to introduce the anger rules to her:

1. Do not hurt self.
2. Do not hurt others.
3. Do not hurt property.

Jenny had never heard of these rules before and was surprised by them. Her usual response when feeling angry was to physically destroy things, either by cutting them up or burning them; she had never given any thought about what else she could do when she felt angry. Whilst thinking of alternative ways to respond to angry feelings, such as drawing and writing down feelings, Jenny explained that in the last three weeks she hadn't set any fires, which felt 'weird' (her word) because she wasn't really sure what to do with her fingers. I introduced the idea that having an elastic band, some blu tac™ or a stress ball can be helpful as discreet distraction tools and agreed to bring these to our next session. Jenny agreed that she would give some thought about what to do when angry, including thinking of creative activities like drawing and crochet.

Mindful of Jenny's comment to her social worker that setting fires was okay if you had water close to hand, I wanted to discuss with her possible scenarios of what can happen when a fire is set. I thought that the die exercise (see Chapter 7) would best facilitate a conversation on these 'what ifs', but on reflection it was the wrong choice. For whilst Jenny was able to easily think of five possible outcomes when setting fires, she quickly dismissed most of them:

1. Go to jail/get a criminal record.
2. Burn myself.
3. Get a bad school or college record.
4. Lose my friends.
5. My family will hate me.

Jenny rapidly concluded that her family already hated her, she had very few friends and she wouldn't mind getting burnt as long as it wasn't her face. Therefore, most of the possible outcomes didn't concern her. Yet she became very upset at the thought of going to jail and was suddenly worried that the police would find out about the fires she'd already set. By doing this exercise it became clear that things often considered important did not have significance for Jenny as they did not exist for her. The one thing she did have – her physical freedom – caused fear when she contemplated this could also be lost. I assured her that the police would not be getting involved because of fires she had previously set, but gently explained that I couldn't guarantee this wouldn't happen in the future, and I drew the game to a close. Pursuing an activity that is causing upset achieves nothing but the potential for more harm to a child who is already distressed.

From this point onwards in my work with Jenny I decided that all the fire-related activities we would do would be those typically used with younger children. This was not to deny her intelligence but to recognise her emotional age, which due to her years of neglect was much younger than her chronological and intellectual age. Despite being a teenager, Jenny's needs were not to explore the science and realities of fire but to learn how to become safer through more playful, child-like activities. I decided that in our next session I would bring the story of a dragon, a hamster and a boy called Jez (discussed in Chapter 6). When ending the session, I asked Jenny what she needed to do to prepare for our next meeting together: 'Not play with fire and think of things to do when I'm mad'. As I accompanied Jenny back to reception, she said to me, 'I'm kinda proud I haven't set fires for three weeks.' 'Kinda proud? Very proud', I replied.

Session four
Ongoing contact with Mum and the family social worker confirmed there was no new firesetting to report, so session four began with

an emotions sheet to show I was happy at Jenny's progress. She pointed to the same face, and the reading of *Jez's Lucky Day* began in happy, positive spirits. So as not to insult her intelligence with a children's story book, I asked if it would be okay for me to read with her one of my most favourite stories ever. With her permission I read the story aloud and Jenny adored it, making links between herself and Jez – she noticed how Jez doesn't appear to have a dad – and was interested in the safe, boundaried pieces of information the story allowed me to give about myself, namely, that I'm also originally from a town in South Wales and that Jez's school looked exactly like mine did. She responded well to all the fire safety messages the book features. The illustrations further allowed her to accept the idea of what can happen in a fire without the anxiety that previous discussions on this subject had caused.

In terms of her 'homework', Jenny was still thinking of things to do when angry and asked for more time to work on this by herself, agreeing in the meantime to use the blu tac™, elastic bands and the stress ball I gave her as ways to keep her fingers occupied when not playing with fire. I ended the session by drawing the fire safety journey image (explained in Chapter 10) to reinforce the journey we were taking together, a journey that would eventually come to an end. When asking Jenny to consider where we were in our journey, she considered herself to be at a mid-way point between previously setting fires and no longer setting fires. She explained that she had often felt unable to control whether or not she set fires. I thanked her for telling me and we agreed that we'd discuss this next time.

Session five

Over a bag of tangerines, we discussed our mutual feelings of pride that there had been no further firesetting. With the routine of discussing feelings now an established part of our work, I introduced Jenny to the wider concept of thoughts-feelings-actions.

I wanted her to be able to challenge her feelings of being unable to control her firesetting. Mapping out on a piece of paper the circular continuum of thoughts-feelings-actions, I illustrated how thoughts influence feelings, which influence our actions.

Jenny found this concept absolutely fascinating because she had thought that she just did things without having any control over them. The realisation that she had the power over her actions by altering how she thought was hugely exciting to her. She talked about a clip she had seen on social media involving a fight between three people on a bus and used the thoughts-feelings-actions approach for each of the people involved. She imagined what each person had been thinking and feeling before they acted. I then asked Jenny to imagine new thoughts and new feelings for each person, which led to her reaching different, non-violent outcomes. Jenny decided this approach was going to help her when she wanted to set a fire and when she became angry; she would recognise the feelings, think differently about them and ultimately act differently. It was a beautifully empowering moment to be a part of.

The session ended with Jenny showing me the rules she had written to accompany our fire safety journey:

1. No lighters.
2. No matches.
3. No candles.
4. Tell the truth.
5. No joking about fire.
6. Have fun.

Jenny had written rule number five because people would taunt her about setting fires. I assured her we'd never joke about the setting of fires. What we were going to do was expand her rules to create a fire safety club in the next session.

Session six

After checking in on how we were feeling over our customary fruit and a Babybel™, Jenny began the fire safety club exercise (see Chapter 6). She clearly relished the opportunity to be as imaginative as possible, creating the club rules, logo (an angel bird) contract, fee, challenges, meeting times, venue and dress code; this was one impressive fire safety club that she proudly named 'The Avoiders of Flames'. (I couldn't help but feel just a wee bit chuffed and proud that the acronym for the club was TAF, which is similar to the nickname 'Taff' for Welsh people.)

Jenny's rules for the club were all linked to fire safety and not setting fires, which is the genius of this activity. Children and teenagers are much less likely to break rules that they have devised and written themselves. The final exercise of the session was to discuss each of Jenny's rules, checking that she understood why it was important to be fire safe. Jenny's homework was to draw the TAF club badge, poster and logo. At the end of the session, Jenny said she felt very proud of herself regarding fire safety and that she was also 'getting better' (her words) in other things. I couldn't help but feel just a wee bit chuffed and proud at that, too.

Session seven

Jenny was waiting for me in school reception ahead of our session, working on a beautiful crocheted blanket. I asked her if she would teach me how to crochet in a future session, to which she agreed and advised I needed to bring a 3.5mm needle and some wool. This was suddenly sounding serious and I wondered what I'd let myself in for.

What children have taught me

Letting children and teenagers teach new things to adults can be a huge boost to their confidence and self-esteem, helping

---

change the power balance where knowledge seemingly only sits with the grown-ups in charge. Eight-year-old Milo used to love teaching me the latest card games he'd learned from his grandfather and the lyrics to songs he'd been singing on his 'okeycokey' [karaoke] machine. I'm also very happy for teenagers to update me on the latest trends, music and technological gadgets, not to mention what new words in their vocabulary mean, because otherwise I'd have absolutely no idea. But let it remain *their* music and *their* words; flossing (the dance) and the word 'sick' is strictly for use by the youth if you want to avoid looking like an idiot. D'ya get me?

As we started the session, I swapped the energy drink Jenny was drinking for the fruit juice I'd bought her. (I poured the energy drink down the sink after the session. It doesn't take a nutritionist to understand that high doses of caffeine and sugar are not the ways to nurture the brain and body ready for a day of learning.) Jenny proudly produced the homework she had prepared – an angel bird logo and badge for her fire safety club – and declared triumphantly that she hadn't set any further fires.

Jenny looked extremely pale and tired during the session, which was pretty remarkable for a girl who was always pale and tired, and described in one child protection meeting as 'incredibly neglected'. None of the concerns since my first home visit had lessened over the five months of working with her but became ever-heightened as Jenny spoke more freely to her social worker, school child protection officer, family therapist and me about home and family life. Jenny's commitment to school and her fire safety journey is made all the more remarkable considering she still lived daily in an abusive home whilst psychotherapy, protection plans, professionals' meetings and legal care proceedings dragged on. If processes are achingly slow for the professionals involved in the decision making, what does it feel like to be the child?

Acknowledging her tiredness, I suggested the session was spent creating a range of fire safety posters for her club. As she drew, we reminded ourselves of the fire safety club rules and why it was important to never set fires. I was curious to know what sanctions Jenny would impose on any club member found breaking the rules. As with many other children I've worked with that have experienced violence, Jenny's sanctions involved harsh physical punishments and as she described them she began to speak about the times she had been frightened by violence at home. This highlights why we must always let children and teenagers draw, doodle and colour during our sessions. Liberated by the lack of eye contact that colouring allows, words can flow like ink from their felt tip pens.

Session eight

Jenny was quiet and withdrawn at the start of the session; having had little sleep and no breakfast she was feeling hungry. Confirming Jenny had no allergies, I gave her all the fruit and snacks I had in my bag (no doubt breaking a number of policies but I was more concerned with the 'let's not have a kid starve to death' policy at that exact moment in time). It was little surprise when Jenny pointed to the emotions 'exhausted', 'depressed', 'frightened' and 'anxious' in our usual checking-in routine. I told Jenny I would let her teacher know how she was feeling, and also speak to her social worker.

What I knew at this point, but Jenny didn't, was that legal proceedings to remove her from the family home had begun. My court report outlining the numerous concerns for her physical and emotional safety had been submitted. I had also been asked to include why I didn't consider Jenny's previous firesetting to be a presenting risk, and that secure accommodation was not required when considering her new placement.

As we began our session, Jenny placed on her hand a sock puppet she had made called Annabella. I spoke to Annabella, commenting it was nice to meet her, that I was glad she was joining us for the session and how I was very worried about Jenny feeling so sad and tired. I asked Annabella if she would like to see all of Jenny's fire safety work to date, which I had laminated and placed in a large red folder. Annabella nodded and Jenny was delighted to see her work presented so carefully and neatly. Jenny was also chuffed to know that the staff in the print-room had printed her angel bird logo on especially thick paper, because they thought it was so beautiful (that same picture remains on my fridge door to this very day). As Jenny was feeling stiff and aching we did some gentle stretching exercises together as we talked, for a less tense body will allow for a more relaxed conversation.

Jenny produced a revised set of anger rules she had written and asked me to place them in her fire safety folder. Her rules read:

'It's okay to feel angry but think...

- Don't hurt others.
- Don't hurt yourself.
- Don't hurt property.
- Do talk about it.'

Jenny explained that she was trying to follow these rules when she got 'mad' (her word) and she was now able to use her imagination instead of setting fires but that she still felt a failure. I gently asked Jenny if it is a failure to be able to crochet? To draw angel birds? To design fire safety clubs? She slowly smiled and gently shook her head. I then introduced her to cinquains (see Appendix VII) for no one who can write poetry is a failure.

Within minutes she produced the following five-line poems:

Photographs
Wales   Countries
Photographing   Walking   Describing
Different areas and animals
Fashion

Laughter
Joy   Happiness
Playing   Laughing   Happy
Love to all people
Families

Winter
Winter-dogs   Spring-cats
Laughing   Shouting   Playing
The joy with winter
Fun

Jenny was impressed with how quickly she could write poetry and our session ended with her offering to write more as homework, which she did by the page-load. Jenny was eager to have another tool to use as a coping mechanism when she felt angry or when she didn't know what to do with her hands, as her mother had removed her stress ball. On learning this, I agreed I would make a 'fiddle kit' for Jenny, a bag of different items that she could use to 'self soothe' when needing distraction from worrying or sad thoughts.

Jenny's fiddle kit
Jenny's fiddle kit was a red cloth drawstring bag with a note in it that read:

'In this bag you will find safe things to play with that can help keep your fingers busy. These are:

- A ball of blu tac™ – what shapes can you make?
- Elastic bands – how does it feel when you pull and stretch them?
- A stress ball – is it easy or difficult to squeeze the ball with one hand?
- A magnet – does the magnet feel cool or warm to touch?
- A keyring – does it feel soft or itchy?
- Paper to draw on; scrunch up; design a new hair accessory; paint a flag for TAF club.
- What else can you do? Crochet? Make a model? Create a new sock puppet?'

Session nine

Jenny and I met in the days following her being placed in the care of her great aunt. I acknowledged that I knew what had happened, and that the session could be as short as Jenny needed if it was difficult to concentrate. She was happy to meet as usual and we spent the hour quietly revisiting fire safety work previously completed, reminding ourselves of all the different fire safety messages Jenny had learned along the way. She drew out our fire safety journey, which she called her 'map from unsafe to safe'. Towards the end of the session we shared a chocolate dessert in celebration of Jenny's recent birthday.

Session ten

Jenny looked noticeably healthier, with clean, shiny hair, colour to her cheeks and more weight. I commented that she looked fantastic and she replied, 'I feel fantastic.' I had brought a crochet needle and Jenny taught me to crochet. I can knit, but I found this the most ridiculously difficult thing I have ever tried and it made me realise all the more just how remarkably talented and clever Jenny is. Despite my incompetence, she was calm, patient and kind about my efforts. With no further firesetting reported and Jenny now in a safe place, I explained that the next three sessions would be preparation for the end of our work, in the form of a collage that captured our fire safety journey. Jenny liked the idea of a collage and agreed to prepare story boards depicting our fire safety journey.

Session eleven

Jenny arrived at the session with two story boards of ideas for her collage. We agreed that the collage and all her fire safety work would be presented in a 'show and tell' at school for selected family members and professionals chosen by Jenny. Talking about the story boards and collage allowed for both reflective and current conversations on fire safety, with Jenny stating she no longer liked to talk about her past firesetting with anyone but me. It appeared that Jenny's firesetting was a chapter in her life she was ready to end and she looked forward to celebrating all that she had achieved in becoming fire safe.

Session twelve

A happy, healthy and confident Jenny began work on her collage. As Jenny chose the images, I helped stick them to the paper in the order she requested, asking what certain images meant and their significance. It was incredible that Jenny remembered conversations we'd had over a year ago, whilst her sense of mischief was also captured; she knew I was a vegetarian and stuck a picture of a great big sausage sandwich in the collage. I quietly thought, 'Yes! Despite everything, this girl knows her own mind and won't be told what to think.' As homework, Jenny had designed invites for her show and tell, which I agreed to send out. Jenny's nan, great aunt, social worker, school child protection officer, psychotherapist and two members of my team were among the invited attendees. Jenny was still undecided about inviting her mother.

Session thirteen

Over fruit, work continued on Jenny's collage as words and pictures depicting her fire safety journey were added. Every image related to fire safety, emotions or a conversation we had, other than a picture of Benedict Cumberbatch as Sherlock Holmes. When asked the significance of Benedict Cumberbatch, Jenny simply looked at me and said, 'It's Benedict Cumberbatch.' Jenny had started work on a long piece of crochet work that would border the collage and she was gracious enough to include my crochet efforts in the picture, too. It was understood that our next session would be our final one-to-one meeting, with the show and tell to follow four months later.

Session fourteen

Jenny's collage was now 55cm by 120cm, and running diagonally through its centre was a painted path that started in red and turned orange, which bled into yellow that became grey and eventually black. Along the path were footsteps depicting the journey from setting fires to no more fires. At the start of the path were words such as 'no safety' and 'trouble' alongside pictures of fire, matches and lighters, but as the path progressed words such as 'I am team Wales', 'protect', 'happy' and 'I am free' appeared alongside images of emotion icons, shooting stars, the Olympic torch and food (although not one piece of fruit!). It was, and is, a powerful and wonderful piece of art that I am incredibly honoured to have seen from start to finish.

We acknowledged that it was sad to be saying goodbye after so many months of working together but we were united in our pride at all Jenny had achieved and the many changes that had taken place. We agreed that the 'show and tell' would be a cause for celebration and that the end of our work was a good thing. Jenny was finally safe.

Fire safety 'show and tell'

Jenny and I met an hour before the 'show and tell' hosted at her school. As we hung her work on the walls where the presentation was to take place, she happily told me all her news from the previous three months, including her first Christmas living with her great aunt. We practised her speech and she showed me the thank you note she had prepared for everyone attending:

> This 'show and tell' was about how we fought and won the battle against fire. Thank you for coming to our 'show and tell'.

Jenny had made the decision to invite her mum to the event, who was joined in the audience by the school child protection officer and two members of my team. Jenny was nervous as the presentation began but did brilliantly, explaining all the fire safety messages she had learned, offering fire safety advice to the audience, talking about the images she had created and even being brave enough to answer questions. After thanking everyone for coming, our work was done. My work was done. Jenny and I said goodbye for what I thought was the final time.

Re-uniting with Jenny

It is very unusual to have any further contact with children once my work has ended. To stay in contact once a case is closed would blur the boundaries of the relationship and potentially send mixed messages; why do I still need to be there if the firesetting no longer presents as a concern? Therefore, there should have been no further contact with Jenny, especially as two months after our work ended I left the London Fire Brigade. Yet life has a funny way of working out sometimes.

At a child protection training course I was attending four years later, Jenny's school child protection officer walked through the door. In a city where 13 million people work, Jenny's school child protection officer and I were on the same training course. Within minutes our conversation turned to Jenny, who I learned was waiting to start the first year of her photography degree. Proud? And some. Happy? It doesn't even come close. In that moment I became my own heart exercise of absolute joy. In our conversations we agreed that Jenny would be the perfect speaker at a UK juvenile firesetter conference I was hosting and chairing later that year, where Professor Kolko was the keynote presenter.

Via the school I sent a letter to Jenny inviting her to speak at the conference and whilst I was on a 'Save the NHS' march in central London a few days later, her email buzzed through to my phone confirming that she would be delighted to speak. Not only did she wow the conference delegates with her eloquence and bravery as she discussed her past firesetting but I feel blessed to be a part of her life again. She lets me know how she's getting on at university and as for me, well, I just couldn't be prouder of her for all that she is and all that she has become.

In conclusion

If it appears that I have glossed over the child protection details of this case, paying lip service to the hundreds of hours of work, worry, phone calls, reports and meetings that went into it, it is out of respect to Jenny's privacy and that of her mother and family. Whilst Jenny has consented to this chapter being written and has helped me to remember much of the information, I have shared only those details that provide an insight into her firesetting and the fire safety work we did together. The rest of Jenny's story is for her to tell, if and when she chooses to.

CHAPTER 10

Endings

From the moment we first start thinking about meeting a child or young person, we are focused on nurturing a trusting relationship built around their safety and the creation of a space where they can play, explore, learn and be heard. Our conscious efforts to create this supportive, positive experience must be as present at the end of our work as they are in the beginning. This is especially vital given that many of the children and teenagers we work with will never have experienced good endings. Just as we give the child or teenager we are working with a five-minute 'flag' to remind them that our session time is soon coming to an end, so we must provide plenty of advance warning about when we are parting for good. Indeed, it can often be helpful to set out from the very first meeting together that our fire safety work will have an end point. To help illustrate this, I turn again to my trusted felt tip pens and coloured paper.

The fire safety journey

Using a pen and a piece of paper, I enable young people to visualise the fire safety journey we are on together by drawing myself and them (stick people will more than do!) at a start sign. Confirming that we are working together until we reach our end point, to symbolise this I draw in the distance a stop sign on the same piece of paper.

Next, I say that the stop sign is usually reached because I have no more fire safety worries, making a point of stressing that I don't see why they should be any different in becoming fire safe. I also say that sometimes I stop because I'm not the best person to help and someone else will support the young person instead (examples of other agencies for onward referral are given in Chapter 8).

From the very beginning this simple drawing allows for a boundary around our work that sets out why we're working together and the journey we're on *together*. As can be seen below and in the drawing I plotted out with David (who we met in Chapter 7), you can return to the journey map during a later session to help identify progress.

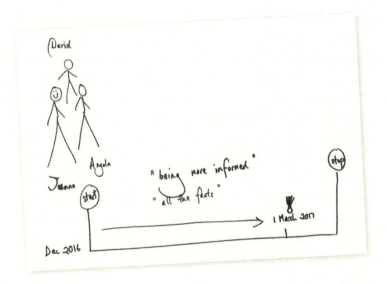

When using the map in this way with David, he saw himself as nearing the end of our work together. When asking the reasons for this he said it was because I had taught him 'stuff' (his word). Being curious about what stuff he meant, he told me that he had learned how quickly fire can develop (through the use of the fire development pictures discussed in Chapter 7) and just how many people it could affect when we completed the ripple exercise (also described in Chapter 7). David's progress was marked on the map and dated, serving as a visible reminder as to how far he'd come (it just so happens that we were meeting on 1 March, St David's Day, and you will see from the drawing that I couldn't resist adding a leek next to the date as it is the national emblem of Wales). Letting a young person see, and reflect on, how far they've come during the fire safety journey can be hugely empowering as they take stock of all the new information they have learned and mastered.

The fire safety collage

For some children and teenagers, and even practitioners, looking ahead to the end of working together can be emotional due to the positive attachments made and another set of changes that lies ahead. Given that even positive changes and endings require planning, the creation of a fire safety collage can really help prepare for the final session and produce a lasting memento of the journey taken together. I never fail to be stunned and humbled by the collages young people create: unique, personal and beautiful pieces of art born out of their creative talent and their interpretation of the fire safety work they have completed. All this is captured via materials that cost virtually nothing other than the time it takes to build a selection of collage materials.

Images from magazines and newspapers, recycled greetings cards, coloured sweet wrappers, buttons, ribbons, pom-poms and pipe cleaners all make for fabulously colourful and tactile collage materials. Be mindful of the magazines and newspapers you use – always checking what is on the reverse of an image you cut out – and ensure you have a range of pictures that can represent the young person and their interests. The following categories can help:

- animals
- travel, the countryside and cities
- fashion

- music and culture
- fire and fire safety, for example a picture of a fire exit sign
- family and people
- food
- anything that the young person has said they particularly like (remember Jenny and Benedict Cumberbatch in Chapter 9!).

Collages are a staple of how I end my long-term work with children and young people because they allow the physical marking of a goodbye brought about by their 'graduation' into a safer place. Criminologist Shadd Maruna (2011) emphasises the importance of rituals and rites of passage for engendering a sense of belonging, so let's ensure we incorporate these into our fire safety endings, especially when they capture and celebrate so powerfully all that has been achieved by our young people.

Fire safety rites of passage

Family fire safety project

Similar to the activities of becoming a Fire Safety Officer (Chapter 6) and creating a fire safety 'show and tell' (Chapter 9), Kolko and Vernberg (2017) encourage the whole family to create a fire safety project together. This shared exercise allows for the child and their parents or carers to get creative together. Producing a piece of work that reflects what they have learned provides a visual, lasting memory of all that they achieved as a united team working together.

Fire station visits

A visit to a fire station at the end of your fire safety work is a way for all the family to re-cap and celebrate all the fire safety lessons that have been learned by everyone in the home. With advance warning and the appropriate permissions granted (in other words please don't just rock up at your local fire station unannounced), fire crews are usually very welcoming of children and teenagers who have learned how to become fire safe. Every child and teenager I work with receives a certificate during our final session together: a permanent and official reminder of all their hard work, effort and achievements. Is it possible that the fire officer in charge of the station you are visiting could present the certificate to the child and young person? I have seen many children rise to the occasion and stand smartly to attention (without being asked) as their certificate is awarded. It's a magical moment.

Re-visiting the heart exercise

If I have used the heart exercise (see Chapter 7) in my work, for the final session I will prepare a heart in advance of the meeting. I will use cut-out images and words on the heart I have drawn to reflect my emotions of pride and joy at all that the young person has achieved. I will also include an image that reminds me of something they said in our work together, along with a hopeful message for the future. This is the heart I prepared and gave to 13-year-old David in our last session together:

Cake and cards

As an end celebration, find out what a child or teenager's favourite cake is and in your last session enjoy a well-deserved slice together (there's a cake to suit every taste, allergy, intolerance and dietary requirement). Finally, consider writing a card thanking them for all they have done and wishing them well. Remembering something mentioned during sessions means you can give a well-thought-out card; mine have included the Mona Lisa, Audrey Hepburn, a dog in a sheriff's hat and a fire engine (of course). Long after we have left, a card can be kept in a drawer or pinned to a noticeboard to be read again and again. Seven years on, Jenny (seen in Chapter 9) tells me she still has the card I gave her during our final meeting together.

Suggestions for giving positive feedback and approval

Non-verbal signs using body language or physical actions

- Smiling
- Pat on the back
- Putting your arm around your child and/or giving them a hug (for parents/families only)
- Giving a 'thumbs up'
- A head nod or a wink
- Clapping your hands
- Others?

Verbal praise

- 'I really like it when you...'
- 'What you just did was wonderful'
- 'Great job!'
- 'Terrific!'
- 'Fabulous!'
- 'What a nice thing to do...'
- 'You did that all by yourself...well done'
- I am so proud of you for...'
- Others?

(Taken from Assessment and Intervention with Children and Adolescents Who Misuse Fire, *Kolko and Vernberg 2017, p.47)*

NFPA® Sparky® activities

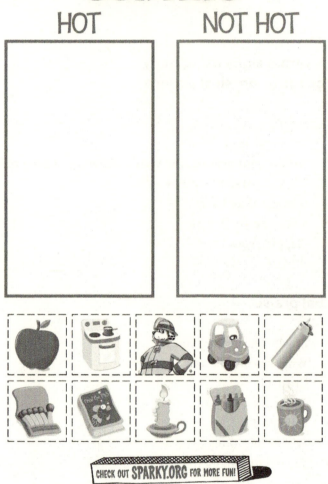

SORTING

| HOT | NOT HOT |

CHECK OUT SPARKY.ORG FOR MORE FUN!

THE NAME AND IMAGE OF SPARKY ARE TRADEMARKS OF THE NFPA.

BOOKMARK BONANZA

SPARKY SAYS:
MAKE SURE
YOUR HOME
HAS WORKING
SMOKE ALARMS.

SPARKY SAYS:
MAKE SURE
YOUR HOME
HAS WORKING
SMOKE ALARMS.

How To Fold An Origami Dog!

You'll need a square piece of paper. If you don't have origami paper, you can make a square from a rectangle. Fold on the dotted lines, and cut away the extra.

remove this part

Fold your square in half diagonally.

Rotate the triangle so the longest edge is at the top.

Fold the top points down on the dotted lines to make ears.

Fold the bottom points up on the dotted line to make a mouth.

Draw a face and spots on your dog to look like Sparky!

Questions for tumbling tower

1. Do you live in a house or a flat?
2. What colour are your kitchen walls?
3. Tell me about your favourite animal.
4. Name your favourite film.
5. Who is your favourite person on television?
6. What food do you like to eat the most?
7. What music makes you feel better when you listen to it?
8. Do you have any pets?
9. What do you do in your free time?
10. What do you like to do at school?
11. If you could have dinner with anyone, who would it be?
12. What job would you like to do in the future?
13. What time of the day is better – morning, afternoon, evening or night?
14. What is your favourite comfort food?
15. If you could visit anywhere in the world, where would it be?
16. Do you have any brothers and sisters?
17. Complete the sentence to say something positive about yourself, 'I am...'
18. Who is your best friend?
19. If you are worried about something, who can you talk to?
20. What book did you read last?
21. Are there any local clubs for young people in your area?
22. Which are better, cats or dogs?
23. Do you like playing or watching sport?

24. Do you usually go to bed early or late?
25. Where is your nearest fire station?
26. What are the three parts of the fire triangle?
27. Where are the smoke alarms fitted in your home?
28. How often should you test your smoke alarms?
29. What are the actions to take if your clothes catch fire?
30. Do you need a fire escape plan at school or home?
31. When should you call 999?
32. What questions will the operator ask you if you call 999?
33. After you have charged your mobile phone, what should you do with the charger?
34. If a fire starts, who could be in danger?
35. Name five safe uses of fire.
36. Who could be affected by a car fire?
37. If you see a fire, how does it make you feel?
38. What is the biggest cause of fatal house fires?
39. Name four ways an accidental house fire could start.
40. What must you *never* use to put out a chip pan or oil fire?
41. At night it is good to have a bedtime routine for fire safety. What could it include?
42. Have you ever visited a fire station?
43. Have you ever thought about working for the fire service?
44. What jobs do you imagine there are in your local fire service?
45. What fire safety advice have you learned at school?
46. Complete the sentence 'Crawl under smoke so you don't _ _ _ _ _.'
47. What kills most people in a fire: the flames or the smoke?
48. Do you like fire?

Fire safety quiz

1. What are the three parts of the fire triangle?

   Oxygen   *Fuel*   *Heat*

2. What happens to a fire if one part of the triangle is removed?

   It dies

3. Look at the fire development stills. Write the timings for each photograph.

   15s *2m* *5m* *8m* *8.30m*

4. Put the four stages of fire development in the correct order.

   3   *1*   *4*   *2*

   Fully Ignition Decay Growth
   developed

5. Complete the sentences with the correct word from the following list:

   Smoke Monthly Drop Choke Plan

   - Smoke alarms should be tested *monthly*.
   - If your clothes catch fire you should stop, *drop* and roll.
   - During escape from a fire, crawl under smoke so you don't *choke*.
   - Every home should have an escape *plan*.
   - Most people killed in fires die through *smoke* inhalation.

Graphing technique

Label each emotion or thought here:

● *Sadness*   ✕ *Anger*   ■ *Thoughts about setting fire*   ▲ *Guilt*

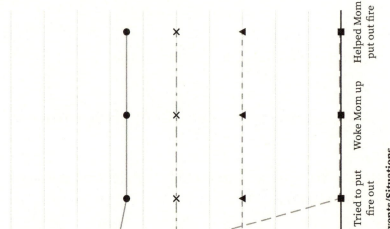

Taken from *Assessment and Intervention with Children and Adolescents Who Misuse Fire*, Kolko and Vernberg 2017, p.49.

M1 Case Study

In April 2011, a fire at a scrapyard in Mill Hill (North London) closed a 6.5 mile stretch of the M1 motorway for several days and caused £4.5m of damage to the scrapyard.

In addition to the closure of the motorway, homes close to the scrapyard had to be evacuated. An exclusion zone was also set up due to the presence of gas cylinders in the scrapyard and the risk of them exploding. Rail services in and out of London were also disrupted because of the scrapyard fire.

The scrapyard fire took place on a Friday night. That weekend, two FA Cup semi-finals were being held at Wembley (involving football teams from Bolton, Stoke and Manchester) and the London Marathon was taking place on the Sunday.

Over three evenings before the scrapyard fire, a series of fires had been set in the surrounding area by ten teenagers aged 15 to 18 years. The fires involved burning materials found in skips, such as old curtains. Aerosols were used as accelerants in the fires set.

All ten teenagers were arrested and charged with arson, including the scrapyard fire. After a ten-week hearing at Crown Court, the teenagers were found not guilty of the scrapyard fire but guilty of over 20 other counts of arson.

Cinquains

A cinquain is a poem of five lines in the following format:

1. The first line is a **one-word title**, the subject of the poem.
2. The second line is **two adjectives** describing the title/subject.
3. The third line is **three verbs ('doing' words)** about the subject.
4. The fourth line consists of **four words summarising** that subject.
5. The fifth line is a **single-word summary** of the subject.

Example:

Snow
Silent, white
Dancing, falling, drifting
Covering everything it touches
Blanket

Titles for cinquains can include:

School Family Football Holidays Ice cream Dogs Cats

The subject titles are endless and can be adapted to suit your client and session.

References

American Psychiatric Association (2013) *Diagnostic and Statistical Manual of Mental Disorders,* 5th edn. Arlington, VA: American Psychiatric Publishing.

Bainbridge, D. (2009) *Teenagers: A Natural History.* London: Portobello Books.

Barlow, D.H. (2004) 'Psychological treatments.' *American Psychologist 59,* 869–878.

BBC news online (2011) *Shops urged put temporary age limit on matches sale.* 21 October. Accessed on 18/02/2019 at www.bbc.co.uk/news/uk-england-south-yorkshire-15404073

Bottoms, A.E. (2012) 'Developing Socio-Spatial Criminology.' In M. Maguire, R. Morgan and R. Reiner (eds) *The Oxford Handbook of Criminology,* 5th edn. Oxford: Oxford University Press.

Campbell, R. (2014) *Playing with fire.* Fire Analysis and Research Department, National Fire Protection Association. NFPA No. USS17. Quincy, MA: National Fire Protection Association. Accessed on 28/05/2019 at www.nfpa.org/-/media/Files/News-and-Research/Fire-statistics-and-reports/US-Fire-Problem/Fire-causes/oschildplay.ashx?la=en

Carroll, L. (1865) *Alice's Adventures in Wonderland.* London: Macmillan Publishers.

Chen, Y., Arria, A.M. and Anthony J.C. (2003) 'Firesetting in adolescence and being aggressive, shy and rejected by peers: New epidemiologic evidence from a national sample survey.' *Journal of the American Academy of Psychiatry 40*, 581–586.

Cooper, M. (2013) *Mini and Me*. London: Ziji Publishing.

Corcoran, S. (2019) *Anger as yobs set fire to Orchard Park beauty spot that's not even open yet*. 15 February. Accessed on 28/05/2019 at www.hull dailymail.co.uk/news/hull-east-yorkshire-news/anger-yobs-set-fire-orchard-2546000

Cotterall, A., McPhee, B. and Plecas, D. (1999) 'Fireplay report: A survey of school-aged youth in grades 1 to 12.' British Columbia: University College of the Fraser Valley (unpublished).

Cousins, L. (2009) *Maisy's Fire Engine*. London: Walker Books.

Crow, A. (2019) *The 1975 firebug who torched a church and planned to burn down Fife College*. Accessed on 28/05/2019 at www.fifetoday.co.uk/lifestyle/nostalgia/the-1975-firebug-who-torched-a-church-and-planned-to-burn-down-fife-college-1-4869617

Dadds, M.R. and Fraser, J.A. (2006) 'Fire interest, firesetting and psychopathology in Australian children: A normative study.' *Australian and New Zealand Journal of Psychiatry 40*, 581–586.

de Thierry, B. (2015) *Teaching the Child on the Trauma Continuum*. Guildford: Grosvenor Publishing.

de Thierry, B. (2017) *The Simple Guide to Child Trauma*. London: Jessica Kingsley Publishers.

Del Bove, G., Caprara, G.V., Pastorelli, C. and Paciello, M. (2008) 'Juvenile firesetting in Italy: Relationship to aggression, psychopathology, personality, self-efficacy, and school functioning.' *European Child and Adolescent Psychiatry 17*, 235–244.

DeSalvatore, G. and Hornstein, R. (1991) 'Juvenile firesetting: Assessment and treatment in psychiatric hospitalization and residential placement.' *Child and Youth Care Forum 20*, 2, 103–113.

Dunn, J., Brown, J. and Beardsall, L. (1991) 'Family talk about feeling states and children's later understanding of others' emotions.' *Developmental Psychology 27*, 3, 448–455.

Franklin, G.A., Pucci, P.S., Arbabi, S., Brandt, M., Wahl, W.L. and Taheri, P.A. (2002) 'Decreased juvenile arson and firesetting recidivism after implementation of a multi-disciplinary prevention program.' *The Journal of Trauma 53*, 2, 60–264.

Gannon, T.A., Alleyne, E., Butler, H., Danby, H. *et al.* (2015) 'Specialist group therapy for psychological factors associated with firesetting: Evidence of a treatment effect from a non-randomised trial with prisoners.' *Behaviour Research and Therapy 73*, 42–51.

Gannon, T.A. and Lockerbie, L. (2014) *Firesetting Intervention Programme for Mentally Disordered Offenders (FIP-MO)*. Kent: Centre of Research and Education in Forensic Psychology.

Garland, D. (2001) *The Culture of Control: Crime and Social Order in Contemporary Society*. Oxford: Oxford University Press.

Hanlon, M. (2009) *The making of a fire-starter: Why arsonists are usually male, young and poor*. 10 February. Accessed on 28/05/2019 at www.dailymail.co.uk/news/article-1140462/The-making-starter-Why-arsonists-usually-male-young-poor.html

Haughton, C. (2012) *Oh No, GEORGE!* London: Walker Books.

Haynes, L., Service, O., Goldacre, B. and Torgerson, D. (2012) *Test, Learn, Adapt: Developing Public Policy with Randomised Controlled Trials*. London: Cabinet Office – Behavioural Insights Team.

How Do I Feel? (2018) Australia: Hinkler Book.

Kazdin, A.E. and Kolko, D.J. (1986) 'Parent psychopathology and family functioning among childhood firesetters.' *Journal of Abnormal Child Psychology 14*, 315–329.

Kolko, D.J. (1996) 'Education and Counseling for Child Firesetters: A Comparison of Skills Training Programs with Standard Practice.' In E.D. Hibbs and P.S. Jensen (eds) *Psychosocial Treatments for Child and Adolescent Disorders: Empirically Based Strategies for Clinical Practice*. Washington, DC: American Psychological Association.

Kolko, D.J. (2001) 'Efficacy of cognitive-behavioral treatment and fire safety education for firesetting children: Initial and follow-up outcomes.' *Journal of Child Psychology and Psychiatry and Allied Disciplines 42*, 359–369.

Kolko, D.J. (2002) 'Research Studies in the Problem.' In D.J. Kolko (ed.) *Handbook on Firesetting in Children and Youth*. San Diego, CA: Academic Press.

Kolko, D.J. and Foster, J.E. (2017) 'Child and Adolescent Firesetting.' In V.B. Van Hasselt and M.L. Bourke (eds). *Handbook of Behavioral Criminology*. New York, NY: Springer International Publishing.

Kolko, D.J and Kazdin, A.E. (1990) 'Matchplay and firesetting in children: Relationship to parent, marital and family dysfunction.' *Journal of Clinical Child Psychology 19*, 229–238.

Kolko, D.J. and Kazdin, A.E. (1992) 'The Emergence and Recurrence of Child Firesetting: A One-Year Prospective Study.' *Journal of Abnormal Child Psychology 20*, 1, 17–37.

Kolko, D.J. and Vernberg, E.M. (2017) *Assessment and Intervention with Children and Adolescents Who Misuse Fire*. New York, NY: Oxford University Press.

Kolko, D.J., Watson, S. and Faust, J. (1991) 'Fire safety/prevention skills training to reduce involvement with fire in young psychiatric inpatients: Preliminary findings.' *Behaviour Therapy 22*, 269–284.

Lambie, I., Seymour, F. and Popaduk, T. (2012) 'Young people and caregivers' perceptions of an intervention program for children who deliberately light fires.' *Evaluation and Program Planning, 35*, 445–452.

Lambie, I., Ioane, J. and Randell, I. (2016) 'Understanding Child and Adolescent Firesetting.' In R. Doley, G.L. Dickens and T.A. Gannon (eds) *The Psychology of Arson*. Abingdon: Routledge.

Lambie, I., Ioane, J., Randell, I. and Seymour, F. (2013) 'Offending behaviours of child and adolescent firesetters over a 10-year follow-up.' *Journal of Child Psychology and Psychiatry 54*, 1295–1307.

Lambie, I. and Randell, I. (2011) 'Creating a firestorm: A review of children who deliberately light fires.' *Clinical Psychology Review 31*, 3, 307–327.

Lambie, I., Randell, I. and McDowell, H. (2013) '"Inflaming your neighbors": Copycat firesetting in adolescence.' *International Journal of Offender Therapy and Comparative Criminology 2014 58*, 9, 1020–1032.

Lasden, M. (1987) 'Stopping the fire starters.' *Hippocrates 1*, 10, 86–87.

Longfield, A. (2018) *The Observer*, 26 August, 2018. Accessed on 27/07/19 at www.theguardian.com/society/2018/aug/25/end-battery-hen-existence-in-summer-holidays-childrens-commissioner

Martin, G., Bergen, H., Richardson, A.S., Roegar, L. and Allinson, S. (2004) 'Correlates of firesetting in a community sample of young adolescents.' *Australian and New Zealand Journal of Psychiatry* 38, 148–154.

Martinson, R. (1974) 'What works? Questions and answers about prison reform.' *The Public Interest 35*, 22–54.

Maruna, S. (2011) 'Re-entry as a rite of passage.' *Punishment & Society 13*, 1, 3–28.

Mehregany, D.V. (1993) 'Firesetting in children.' *Jefferson Journal of Psychiatry 11*, 2, 18–28.

Ministry of Education (2015) *Special Educational Needs and Disability Code of Practice: 0 to 25 Years. Statutory guidance for organisations which work with and support children and young people who have special educational needs or disabilities.* London: HMSO.

Ó Ciardha, C., Tyler, N. and Gannon, T.A. (2017) 'Pyromania.' In S. Goldstein and M. DeVries (eds) *Handbook of DSM-5 Childhood Disorders.* New York, NY: Springer International Publishing.

Palmer, E.J., Caulfield, L.S. and Hollin, C.R. (2005) *Evaluations of Interventions with Arsonists and Young Firesetters.* London: Office of the Deputy Prime Minister.

Peppa Pig: The Fire Engine (2010) London: Penguin.

Piaget, J. (1936) *Origins of Intelligence in the Child.* London: Routledge & Kegan Paul.

Pinsonneault, I.L. (2002) 'Fire Safety Education and Skills Training.' In D.J. Kolko (ed.) *Handbook on Firesetting in Children and Youth.* California: Academic Press.

Roddie, S. (2006) *Colour Me Happy.* London: Macmillan Publishers.

Slavkin, M.L. and Fineman, K. (2000) 'What every professional who works with adolescents needs to know about firesetters.' *Adolescence 35*, 759–773.

Stadolnik, R.F. (2000) *Drawn to the Flame: Assessment and Treatment of Juvenile Firesetting Behaviour.* Sarasota, FL: Professional Resource Press.

Swain-Bates, C. (2013) *Big Hair, Don't Care.* Walnut, CA: Goldest Karat Publishing.

Vygotsky, L.S. (1926) 'Imagination and creativity in childhood.' Reproduced in 2004 in *Journal of Russian and East European Psychology 42,* 1, 7–97.

Webb, N.B., Sakheim, G.A. and Towns-Miranda, L. (1990) 'Collaborative treatment of juvenile firesetters: Assessment and outreach.' *American Journal of Orthopsychiatry 60,* 2, 305–310.

Weisburd, D., Groff, E.R. and Yang, S-M. (2012) *The Criminology of Place: Street Segments and Our Understanding of the Crime Problem.* Oxford: Oxford University Press.

Weisz, J.R. and Kazdin, A.E. (2017) *Evidence-Based Psychotherapies for Children and Adolescents,* 3rd edn. New York, NY: Guilford.

Wikström, P-OH., Oberwittler, D., Treiber, K. and Hardie, B. (2012) *Breaking Rules: The Social and Situational Dynamics of Young People's Urban Crime.* Oxford: Oxford University Press.

Wooden, W. and Berkey, M.L. (1984) *Children and Arson: America's Middle Class Nightmare.* New York, NY: Plenum.

Zolotow, C. (1972) *William's Doll.* New York, NY: HarperCollins Publishers.

Further Reading

The following lists are by no means exhaustive given the plethora of books that are available on each given topic. However, these are the books that either help me to be a better practitioner or without which I couldn't do my job. Often it's both.

Firesetting behaviour

Cooper, M. (2013) *Mini and Me.* London: Ziji Publishing.

Dickens, G.L., Sugarman, P.A. and Gannon, T.A. (eds) (2012) *Firesetting and Mental Health.* London: RCPsych.

Doley, M.R., Dickens, G.L. and Gannon, T.A. (eds) (2016) *The Psychology of Arson: A Practical Guide to Understanding and Managing Deliberate Firesetters.* London: Routledge.

Kolko, D.J. (ed.) (2002) *Handbook on Firesetting in Children and Youth.* San Diego, CA: Academic Press.

Kolko, D.J. and Vernberg, E.M. (2017) *Assessment and Intervention with Children and Adolescents Who Misuse Fire.* New York, NY: Oxford University Press.

Sagar, R. (1999) *Hull, Hell and Fire: The Extraordinary Story of Bruce Lee.* Beverley: Highgate Publications.

Wooden, W.S. and Berkey, M.L. (1984) *Children and Arson: America's Middle Class Nightmare.* New York, NY: Plenum Press.

Other behaviours and topics
Anger
Whitehouse, E. and Pudney, W. (1996) *A Volcano in My Tummy*. Gabriola Island, BC: New Society Publishers.

Anxiety
Eastham, C. (2017) *We're All Mad Here*. London: Jessica Kingsley Publishers.

Farnsworth, L. (ed.) (2014) *Creative Therapy Colouring Book'* London: Michael O'Mara Books.

Ironside, L. and Ironside, H. (2015) *Colour Away Your Worries*. London: Buster Books.

Ironside, V. (2015) *The Huge Bag of Worries*. London: Hodder and Stoughton.

Autism
Gerland, G. (1997*) Finding Out about Asperger Syndrome, High Functioning Autism and PDD*. London: Jessica Kingsley Publishers.

Haddon, M. (2004) *The Curious Incident of the Dog in the Night-Time*. London: Vintage.

Welton, J. (2004) *Can I tell you about Asperger Syndrome?* London: Jessica Kingsley Publishers.

Choices
Haughton, C. (2012) *Oh no, GEORGE!* London: Walker Books.

Courage and peer pressure
Gulliford, L. (2019) *Can I tell you about Courage?* London: Jessica Kingsley Publishers.

Depression
Ironside, V. (2003) *The Wise Mouse*. London: Young Minds.

Stevens, L. (2016) *Not Today, Celeste!* London: Jessica Kingsley Publishers.

Direct work

Oaklander, V. (1988) *Windows to Our Children*. New York, NY: Gestalt Development.

Tait, A. and Wosu, H. (2016) *Direct Work with Family Groups: Simple, Fun Ideas to Aid Engagement and Assessment and Enable Positive Change*. London: Jessica Kingsley Publishers.

Disability

Todd, P. (2001) *It's Okay to Be Different*. New York, NY: Little, Brown and Company.

Domestic abuse

Doyle, R. (1996) *The Woman Who Walked into Doors*. London: Random House.

Empathy

Lawson, J.A. (2015) *Footpath Flowers*. London: Walker Books.

Families

Todd, P. (2003) *The Family Book*. New York, NY: Little, Brown and Company.

Feelings

Foster, J. (2000) *I'm in a Mood Today: Poems about Feelings*. Oxford: Oxford University Press.

Harper, A. (2015) *It's Not Fair!* Dorking: Bonnier Publishing.

Law, D. (2016) *Secret, Secret*. London: Jessica Kingsley Publishers.

Roddie, S. (2006) *Colour Me Happy*. London: Macmillan Publishers.

Friendship

Barnard, S. (2016) *Beautiful Broken Things*. London: Macmillan Publishers.

Bourne, H. (2015) *Am I Normal Yet?* London: Usborne Publishing.

Grief and loss

Rosen, M. (2004) *Michael Rosen's Sad Book*. London: Walker Books.

Identity and diversity

Byers, G. (2018) *I Am Enough*. New York, NY: HarperCollins Publishers.

Fierstein, H. (2002) *The Sissy Duckling*. New York, NY: Aladdin Paperbacks.

Swain-Bates, C. (2013) *Big Hair, Don't Care*. Walnut, CA: Goldest Karat Publishing.

Zolotow, C. (1972) *William's Doll*. New York, NY: HarperCollins Publishers.

Schizophrenia

Filer, N. (2014) *The Shock of the Fall*. London: Borough Press.

Selective mutism

Winter, T. (2017) *Being Miss Nobody*. London: Usborne Publishing.

Social change

Jones, S. (ed.) (2018) *Thirty Years of Social Change*. London: Jessica Kingsley Publishers.

Trauma

de Thierry, B. (2017) *The Simple Guide to Child Trauma*. London: Jessica Kingsley Publishers.

Organisations, Helplines and Websites Offering Support and Advice

Fire and Rescue Services

UK Fire and Rescue Services provide juvenile firesetter intervention services to their local communities, and the fitting of free smoke alarms in homes where children are setting fires. To access these services, contact your local Fire and Rescue Service. A list of all UK Fire and Rescue Services and their contact details can be found by visiting the Chief Fire Officers Association at www.cfoa.org.uk

National Resources — Firesetting behaviour

fabtic ltd.

fabtic is run by Joanna Foster (this book's author) and specialises in juvenile firesetting behaviour. In addition to working directly with children, teenagers and their families, fabtic also provides training, consultancy and case supervision services to organisations and practitioners supporting children and young people who set fires.

www.fabtic.co.uk
info@fabtic.co.uk
020 7249 0652
@fabtic_ltd

National Resources — Other
ADHD
ADHD Foundation
www.adhdfoundation.org.uk
info@adhdfoundation.org.uk
0151 237 2661

Adoption and fostering
Barnardo's
www.barnardos.org.uk

Autism
National Autistic Society
www.nas.org.uk
nas@nas.org.uk
020 7833 2299

Bereavement
Cruse Bereavement Care
www.cruse.org.uk/get-help/about-grief/about-bereavement
info@cruse.org.uk
Call the Cruse helpline on 0808 808 1677, open Monday to Friday, 9.30am to 5pm (excluding bank holidays), with extended hours on Tuesday, Wednesday and Thursday evenings until 8pm.

Bullying
National Bullying Helpline
www.nationalbullyinghelpline.co.uk
admin@nationalbullyinghelpline.co.uk
Call the National Bullying Helpline on 0845 225 5787, open 9am to 5pm Monday to Friday.

Child poverty
Children's Society
www.childrenssociety.org.uk

Child protection and safeguarding
NSPCC
www.nspcc.org.uk
Children and young people call Childline on 0800 1111.
Adults can call the NSPCC helpline on 0808 800 5000 for concerns about a child.

Child Sexual Exploitation (CSE) and trafficking
NWG Network
www.nwgnetwork.org
network@nwgnetwork.org
01332 585 371

Children in care
Action for Children
www.actionforchildren.org.uk/what-we-do/children-young-people
/support-for-children-in-care

Domestic abuse
Refuge
www.refuge.org.uk
Women's aid
www.womensaid.org.uk

Freephone 24-Hour National Domestic Violence Helpline: 0808 2000 247
Run in partnership between Women's Aid and Refuge

Eating disorders
Beat
www.beateatingdisorders.org.uk
Call their Youthline on 0808 801 0711, open 365 days a year from 12pm to 8pm during the week and 4pm to 8pm on weekends and bank holidays.

Family and parenting
Family Lives (previously known as ParentLine)
www.familylives.org.uk
Call the Family Lives helpline service on 0808 800 2222 for emotional support, information, advice and guidance on any aspect of parenting and family life. Open 9am to 9pm, Monday to Friday and 10am to 3pm Saturday and Sunday.

Feeling scared, lonely or need someone to talk to
Childline
www.childline.org.uk
Call their helpline on 0800 11 11

Samaritans
www.samaritans.org
Call the Samaritans helpline free on 116 123 for free 24 hours a day, 365 days a year.

Female Genital Mutilation (FGM)
Call the NSPCC's FGM helpline on 0800 028 3550 or email fgmhelp@nspcc.org.uk

Food banks
www.trusselltrust.org/get-help/find-a-foodbank
enquiries@trusselltrust.org
01722 580 180

Homelessness
Centre Point
www.centrepoint.org.uk

LGBT+
Switchboard
www.switchboard.lgbt
Call the Switchboard helpline on 0300 330 0630, open every day from 10am to 10pm.

Mental health
Sane
www.sane.org.uk
Call the Sane helpline on 0300 304 7000, open daily from 4.30pm to 10.30pm.

Young Minds
www.youngminds.org.uk
Text the Young Minds Crisis Messenger for free, urgent support across the UK if you are experiencing a mental health crisis. Text YM to 85258. All texts are answered by trained volunteers, with support from experienced clinical supervisors.

Call the Parents Helpline on 0808 802 5544 Monday to Friday 9.30am to 4pm (free for mobiles and landlines).

Parents in prison
PACT
www.prisonadvice.org.uk

Call the PACT prisoners' families helpline on 0808 808 3444 open Monday to Friday from 10am to 5pm.

Self-harm
Selfharm UK
www.selfharm.co.uk
info@selfharm.co.uk

Substance misuse
Turning Point
www.turning-point.co.uk

Transgender
Trans Unite
www.transunite.co.uk

About the Author

Originally from the South Wales Valleys and a history graduate of Oxford University, Joanna Foster has spent the last 16 years working with children and teenagers who set fires, first as Manager of the London Fire Brigade's juvenile firesetters intervention scheme and currently as Managing Director of her own company, fabtic ltd. In the last six years, Joanna has trained fire and rescue service staff from every region across Wales and England along with practitioners from the fields of social care, education, academia, Child and Adolescent Mental Health Services (CAMHS), forensic psychology, the police, secure units, arts therapies, youth justice and Her Majesty's Prison and Probation Service (HMPPS). Joanna's work has been featured in the *Financial Times* and a BBC2 documentary entitled *The Kids That Play with Fire*, and she has presented at conferences in the UK, Ireland, Scandinavia, the USA and New Zealand.

To complement her front-line work, Joanna is currently studying for a master's degree in Applied Criminology, Penology and Management at Cambridge University. In her free time, Joanna can be found contentedly wandering the shelves of children's bookshops, dodging London buses on her bicycle and laughing along to Laurel and Hardy films. And eating. Usually eating.

Index